The
Stove
Book

First published in Great Britain 2014 by
Posthouse Publishing,
26 Peacock Lane, Holt,
Norfolk, NR25 6HA
www.posthousepublishing.com
Volume © Posthouse Publishing 2015
Text © Sune Nightingale 2015

A CIP catalogue for this book is available from the British Library
ISBN 978 1 903872 34 5

10 9 8 7 6 5 4 3 2 1

Printed and bound in Estonia

Author acknowledgements
I would like to thank the many people who have helped me to compile and write this book. My
father John proved an excellent sounding board and wrote some sections, and my mother Susi made
a great number of useful suggestions and additions. As you can tell, we are a stove-obsessed family!
   My thanks go to Lisa Morris for her editing skills and to my publisher Rupert Wheeler and his
team, without whose knowledge and experience this book would never have happened.
   I hope that reading *The Stove Book* enables you to get the best from your wood-burning stove. In
this day and age we need to be turning our back on fossil fuels – and keeping warm from a stove is a
wonderfully enjoyable way to do it.
Sune Nightingale

Picture acknowledgements
The publishers would like to thank all those stove manufacturers who have supplied images. All other
images supplied by Stovesonline except for the following.
© Arada Stoves Ltd pages 11, 15. © PapaPiper page 113.
© Bigstock Photo pages 3, 4, 36, 119, all images on pages (119, 122, 123), 126, 129,
Reproduced with the permission of WCR Property, developers/owners of the first PassivHaus
Offices in England, page 51.

The Stove Book

A complete guide to buying and using a wood-burning stove

Sune Nightingale

Contents

Chapter Four: Installing a stove

Chapter Five: Using a stove

Chapter Six: Firewood and its sources

Introduction

You can't beat the cosy glow and crackle of a wood-burning stove on a cold winter's night. For centuries, people have gathered around fires, not only to keep warm and cook food but also to relax and socialise with others. The mesmeric effect of dancing flames creates an ambiance that a radiator or a gas fire could never aspire to. The sight, smells and sounds of a real fire awaken something primeval within us, reaching back to a time when we felt safe and warm if the fire was there to hold the darkness at bay.

In Britain we've traditionally had open fires in our homes. However, while a fireplace looks great, and keeps us warm if we are sitting in front of it, it is essentially a hole to the outside, sucking warm air out of the house and drawing cold air in as draughts to replenish it. When stoves started to arrive in Britain from the colder Scandinavian countries, they were a revelation. It may seem counter-intuitive that if you put the fire inside a metal box it becomes so much more efficient, but when the first box stoves from the likes of Jøtul came to our shores in the seventies, they burned a fraction of the wood that a fireplace used, could stay in night and day, and spread their warmth right around the house.

Wood-burning stoves have moved on a long way in the last fifty years, giving us unheard-of heights of efficiency, total controllability, stay-clean windows to watch the fire through, and beautiful shapes and colours to please the eye. However, that essential, paradoxical idea is still the same – put the fire in a metal box and it will work a hundred times better.

Today, as we realise the damage that we've done to our planet by burning fossil fuels, those wood-burners have never been so essential. Whether it's a simple stove warming your living room, a wood pellet stove lighting itself on demand or a log gasification boiler with the fire burning upside down, the principle is the same and the fuel is the same. Wood remains a largely carbon-neutral, renewable fuel which is adding less to global warming and grows in abundance on our own little island. The electricity might turn off, the oil can run out or the global gas tap be shut off, but our stoves will continue to work. We will still be able to warm our houses and cook food, and they'll carry on giving us a light in the darkness!

These days there are hundreds of different stoves to choose from;

The wood-burning Esse Ironheart is an example of a cooker stove brought up to date.

different shapes, different sizes, different technologies, and different types of chimney to plug them into. In this book we decipher all the jargon and sort myth from fact. We explain how a stove works, arm you with the knowledge to choose the right stove for your situation, and tell you exactly what is involved in buying and installing a stove.

Once your stove is in place we look at the best wood to burn in it and how to prepare and store those logs. We examine the techniques for lighting the stove easily and how to keep it burning at its best. We troubleshoot any problems that could occur and run through the care and maintenance that your stove and chimney are going to need.

Getting a stove and living with it should be a fun and life-enhancing experience. You don't have to become obsessed like we are but, be warned, many do! Most importantly, by the time you've read this book, you should be more than halfway to becoming an expert on stoves and ready to enjoy the experience of owning your own iron box with flames in.

Sune Nightingale 2014

CHAPTER ONE

How a wood-burning stove works

❝ *Modern wood-burning stoves can burn wood slowly a lot better than earlier models as a result of improved firebox design and cleverly managed air supplies.* ❞

LEFT: *The Hunter Norreskoven is a cleanburning wood-burning stove suitable for smokeless zones.*

9

A stove is reassuringly simple, with few moving parts. In this chapter we run through the main components of a stove so you can become familiar with the terminology used throughout this book as well as understand how each part contributes to the whole.

We look at how heat from a stove is passed to your room, and how this might have a bearing on your choice of stove. We also cover heat storage: most stoves generally only heat the room while they are burning, but it's possible to store up that heat and then release it over longer periods.

Parts of a stove

1. Firebox

The firebox is where your firewood actually burns. A good stove maintains good heat in the firebox and allows you to easily control the burn rate, which helps make the stove effective, efficient and easy to use. Make sure the firebox is the right size for your needs. If you know the size of logs you plan to burn, check that you'll be able to fit them in. If the firebox is too small, you'll have to constantly fill it with twigs; too big and it isn't likely to burn well.

2. Firebricks

Wood burns best in a really hot firebox and so many modern stoves have highly insulating bricks lining the firebox. These reflect the heat of the flames back to the fire so that a high running temperature is quickly reached and maintained. They also protect the stove body from the flame, avoiding the metal being damaged by the heat. Firebricks can be a solid cast material, similar to fired clay, or softer vermiculite, which comes in sheets and can be cut with a suitable saw. Firebricks can be damaged if the stove is refuelled roughly and they are knocked, but you can buy replacement bricks.

3. Baffle or throat plate

The baffle plate (also known as a 'throat' plate) is usually made from metal, but increasingly highly insulating vermiculite baffle plates are being used. The baffle plate rests above the fire, usually at the back of the firebox at a slight angle, blanking off the direct path to the flue

The parts of a typical stove (numbers relate to text)

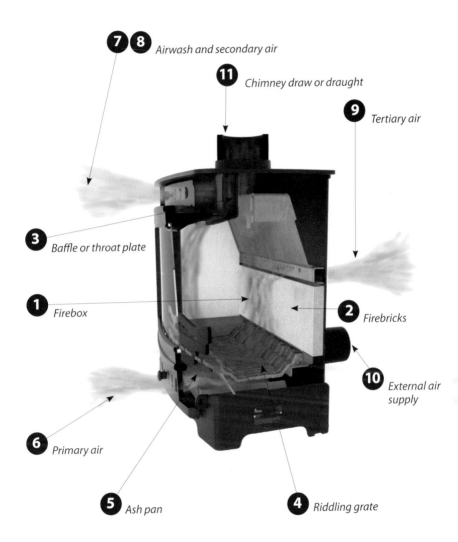

7 8 Airwash and secondary air

11 Chimney draw or draught

9 Tertiary air

3 Baffle or throat plate

1 Firebox

2 Firebricks

10 External air supply

6 Primary air

5 Ash pan

4 Riddling grate

© Arada Stoves

exit. Hot gases from the fire must travel around the baffle plate to reach the flue exit. As they do so, heat from them passes to the metal case of the stove and into the room so you can benefit from the heat. Some stoves have more extensive baffle systems, or a series of baffles, to make the path taken by the hot flue gases even longer, thereby extracting more heat from them. The baffle plate also aids secondary combustion – the burning of flue gases.

4. Grate

A grate forms the base of the firebox and is made up of some form of cast iron plate with slots in it or individual grate bars separated by an air gap. The grate allows air from below to reach the fuel. Grates can be either static (non-moving) or riddling. Riddling is when you agitate the grate to make the ash fall through to the ash pan. This opens up the air gaps again, enabling air to reach the fire. A grate is essential when burning coal, as coal needs air from below to burn well. You should avoid ash building up under the grate, especially when burning coal, as it will cause the grate to overheat, so be sure to empty the ash pan frequently.

Riddling works by moving or shaking the whole grate in some way, by raising alternate grate bars, or by sliding alternate grate bars past each other. An external handle allows you to riddle the grate and this is best done with a little vigour and speed. Although wood burns best with an air supply from above, a grate is a way of providing an air supply from below the fire for when you are first lighting the stove or when you are refuelling. Opening up the primary air vent can give that necessary boost of extra air needed to get the stove going well. Arada and Hunter stoves have a clever flexi-grate so that you can leave the grate open or close it with a handle to form a flat bed for wood burning – thus getting the best of both worlds.

Many wood-burning stoves that have a grate don't have a riddling mechanism, so you simply have to poke at the ash using the tool provided with the stove. Wood burns well on a bed of ash, as the ash forms an insulating layer, which bounces the heat back up into the fire.

Lots of wood-burning stoves have no grate at all. This gains valuable space in the firebox, because as well as the grate there is usually an ash pan under the grate, which takes up room that could otherwise be part of the firebox. This is really important for wood burning because it takes a larger volume of logs to produce the same amount of heat as coal.

5. Ash pan

Most stoves with a grate have an ash pan underneath for collecting ash. The pan usually has a handle, allowing you to pick it up using the tool provided with the stove – but remember that the ash pan and ashes can be hot. It's a good idea to empty the hot ashes into a metal bucket first, allowing them to cool before disposing of them later. Alternatively, some people use an ash carrier – a square box to slide the ash pan into – which can be useful to avoid spilling ashes while carrying them through the house or outside the house, where the wind might otherwise scatter them.

It's fine to put wood ash on the garden or in the compost, as long as you haven't burned treated timber; ash from coal should never be used in this way. In many modern wood-burning stoves, the ash pan has reduced in size and is really there to provide a method of routing and controlling the primary air supply below the grate.

6. Primary air

Primary air is the air fed into the bottom of the firebox. This is either fed up through a grate of some sort, or supplied through air inlets near the bottom of the firebox or in the bottom of the door.

7. Secondary air

Secondary air is air supplied near the top of the firebox. Often it is run through channels in the body of the stove to preheat it, so that when it arrives in the firebox it is hot and doesn't cool the fire down. One of the tricks to make wood combust efficiently is to keep the firebox temperature high. When wood burns it is mainly gases that you can see burning. These gases (predominantly carbon monoxide) are released from the wood and tend to burn above the firebed, so a good supply of air is needed at this higher level.

Balancing the primary and secondary air supplies to the firebox helps to achieve high combustion temperatures, low particulate emissions and optimum efficiency.

8. Airwash

Most modern stoves have what is called an airwash system, whereby a layer of air is sucked over the stove window. This is commonly supplied through a long slot at the top of the window, but it may also be supplied at the base of the window. Quite often the air is preheated by being run through ducts in the body of the stove.

The function of airwash is to help keep the stove window clean. As tars and other deposits from the fire cool, they condense and can accumulate on colder parts of the stove. This occurs particularly when the stove is first lit, being refuelled or burned very slowly. The stove window is often cooler than the rest of the firebox and is the one place where deposited tar is particularly visible. Airwash reduces tarring by providing a protective layer of air, which keeps the flames and gases away from the glass, although some tarring is inevitable. Running the stove in its highest heat mode for a short period burns off most of the tar, and any residue can easily be removed with wood ash or a cleaning pad (*see* page 105). Beware though – a stove window that keeps going black could indicate other problems and is often associated with burning 'wet' wood (*see* Troubleshooting page 100, and *see* The seasoning process page 123).

Airwash also functions as the source of secondary air to the firebox. Many modern stoves have some airwash on all the time, and cannot be turned right down. As a result the window stays clearer for longer and the stove runs more efficiently and produces less smoke.

9. Tertiary air

Some stoves have a tertiary air supply, which remains fixed and cannot be adjusted. Often this is routed through channels in the stove to preheat it. It is usually supplied at the back of the firebox, either through holes in the firebricks or via a horizontal metal strip built in at the base of the baffle plate. When the stove is up to temperature you can see the effect of this air supply, as each air hole appears to have a jet of fire coming out of it. In fact, this jet is the gases from the wood oxidising (burning) when they come into contact with a fresh source of oxygen.

Modern wood-burning stoves can burn wood slowly a lot better than earlier models as a result of improved firebox design and

Primary, secondary and tertiary airflow

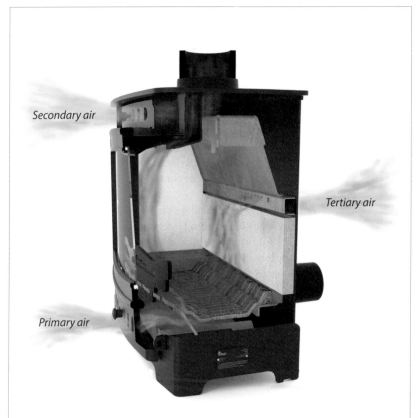

Secondary air

Tertiary air

Primary air

Primary air is used to burn coal and help get a wood fire started. Once the wood is burning properly it is normally closed off.

Secondary air provides the airwash to keep the glass clean and supplies most of the air that is used to keep the wood, and the gases that it gives off, burning.

Tertiary air is preheated as it passes through a heat exchanger chamber within the firebox and is then drawn into the fire, where it combusts unburned hydrocarbons to provide a cleaner burn and greater thermal efficiency.

cleverly managed air supplies. (While you cannot completely turn down the stove, you can usually reduce the air supply so it ticks over comfortably at lower outputs and maintains a good burn.) This produces some amazing flame patterns as well – glowing logs at the base of the firebox and dancing flames hovering above, flickering as the gases catch and burn.

10. External air supply

Stoves are now being made which can be connected to an external air supply, which is essential as our houses become more and more airtight. These vary in that some only supply the primary air for the stove, while others supply 100 per cent of the air needed; it is worth asking about this before you buy.

The fire needs air to burn, and if that air comes from the room in which the stove is located, you may require an air vent directly into the room itself. Although opening up a hole in the outside wall to admit air sounds rather drastic, there are many through-the-wall ventilation kits available that minimise the potential for draughts.

11. Chimney draw or draught

Chimney suction is referred to as draw or draught. The draw from the chimney is what provides the suction needed to move air through the stove. Modern, heavily baffled stoves need a stronger draw to make the stove work well. A well-insulated chimney generally helps to provide a strong and consistent draw.

How a stove heats the room

Heat is passed from the fire inside the stove to the room through a combination of conduction, radiation and convection.

Conduction is the process whereby the heat produced by the fire is conducted through the metal of the stove to the outside of the body. That heat is then pushed into the room by infrared radiation. The hotter the stove becomes the more infrared waves it produces. These are the same waves that travel from the sun to the earth and warm us when it is sunny, which is why we feel warmth on our skin

RIGHT: *Stockton 14HB wood-burning boiler stove.*

when we stand near a stove. Sit in front of a stove so you can feel the heat, hold your hand in front of your face and notice what a large difference it makes. This is simply because you are stopping the radiant heat from reaching your face.

Convection occurs when that radiant heat meets the air and passes some of its heat to it. Air that has been warmed becomes less dense and so rises. This is followed by cooler air, which in turn is warmed, and an air-circulation pattern forms. If you were to release coloured smoke near a stove, you would see the hot air rising from the stove, going across the ceiling, dropping back down to the floor and then back to the stove, spreading the heat through the room as a result. Some stoves, known as convection stoves, are designed to encourage convection. This provides a more even heat to the room and lowers the surface temperature of the stove, which can be an important safety consideration. Convection stoves are discussed in more detail *see* page 26.

Storing heat for later

If you want to store heat so that your stove can provide warmth over an extended period, one option is to have a boiler stove connected to a thermal store. A thermal store is essentially a large-capacity, well-insulated water cylinder that can be interlinked with your boiler stove and central heating system. It allows you to burn your stove relatively hot, so achieving a higher efficiency, and then store the excess heat for use later on.

A thermal store also enables you to easily link your stove with other types of renewable heating, such as solar panels and heat pumps. A wood-burning boiler stove is the perfect partner for a solar heating system, as the solar panels can provide domestic hot water when the stove isn't in use during the summer months, and the stove takes over the job during the winter months when the solar panels have limited effect. Equally heat pumps are efficient when producing low-level hot water but work inefficiently when higher temperatures are needed. So have the heat pump warm the thermal store and then let the stove take it up to full heat.

Another way to store up heat is in masonry, using a masonry stove or Kachelofen (*see* Chapter Two).

RIGHT: *Morsø Panther – a traditional Danish 8kW cast-iron multi-fuel stove.*

CHAPTER TWO

Stove types and accessories

> 66 *Unlike many of their predecessors, contemporary stoves feature large windows to provide a great view of the burning wood. Some models even provide views from three sides.* 99

LEFT: *A Charnwood Country 4 multi-fuel stove.*

21

Modern stoves come in many sizes and styles, and boiler stoves can also provide your hot water and central heating. Some time ago, steel quality was such that there were often problems with steel stoves warping from the heat. But today, whether a stove is made of cast iron or steel is usually not an issue of robustness or quality but rather of aesthetics.

Many UK-manufactured stoves are made of steel, with cast iron used for parts where the heat is intense – the grate, door, flue spigot and sometimes the baffle. Cast-iron stoves are heavier and take longer to heat up and cool down than steel stoves. When heated, cast iron will expand just like steel but tends to be better at keeping its shape as it heats and cools, which is one reason why it is used for stove parts that need to take extreme heat.

The most popular style of stove in the UK is something roughly box-shaped. Previously there may have been rope patterns cast into the doors and latticework over the glass, but nowadays the overall look tends to be simpler, the window larger and the view through the glass unimpeded.

Types of stove

Multi-fuel and wood-burning only

A multi-fuel stove is able to burn a variety of fuels – usually coal, wood and wood briquettes. By 'coal' we mean anthracite, most often available in the form of manufactured ovals. House coal – the big lumpy stuff – while enticingly cheap, is not generally suited for use in stoves, as it is too dirty; and most manufacturers specifically say not to use it or their warranty becomes void. A multi-fuel stove gives you some extra flexibility: if you've run out of wood, you may still have a bag of coal to hand. All multi-fuel stoves have a grate and usually an ash pan, but quite a few wood-burning stoves have neither. To make doubly sure, you can find out if a particular stove is a 'dedicated wood-burner' or 'wood-burning only' – and of course if it lacks a grate and ash pan. Wood is less energy-dense than coal and so more space is

RIGHT ABOVE: *Future Fires FX1 – A British built contemporary 8KW oval wood-burning stove.*
RIGHT BELOW: *The Stovax Riva Studio 1 with black glass top and gloss black enamelled flue pipe is designed as a dedicated wood-burner.*

needed to give out the same amount of heat. So if you're going to burn only wood, then gaining space taken up by the grate and ash pan is a great advantage because you can fit larger pieces of wood in the firebox. This may also mean slightly less cutting, as you can probably use a few longer logs.

Free-standing

Free-standing stoves are available in various shapes and sizes. Boxed or rectangular stoves have been firm favourites for many years in the UK. However, round and oval-shaped stoves as well as stoves mounted on plinths or pedestals are also becoming popular, their design influenced by Scandinavian manufacturers. These are often placed against a plain wall or in the centre of a room, whereas UK traditional box-shaped stoves will often be installed in an existing fireplace opening.

Contemporary

Tall and cylindrical stoves from Scandinavia (especially Denmark) have been gaining appeal. The tall body shape enables flue gases to travel further before passing into the chimney, thus extracting more heat and generally leading to higher efficiencies. Although overall efficiency depends on a number of factors, these tall cylindrical stoves are often well over 75 per cent efficient. Further design improvements may one day result in efficiencies of over 90 per cent, though bear in mind that as the efficiency increases, the amount of heat passing into the chimney reduces, making the design of the chimney ever more important (*see* Chimneys page 68). Many contemporary stoves are designed to have a relatively low heat output to room to make them suitable for modern sealed houses, but a few are in the 8–12kW range.

Unlike many of their predecessors, contemporary stoves feature large windows to provide a great view of the burning wood. Some models even provide views from three sides. Major advances in the materials used for the windows have resulted in high-temperature, shatter-proof 'glass' that can withstand the constant cycling between high and low temperatures, is easy to keep clean and does not normally need replacing in the life of a modern stove.

A word of caution: the 'glass' used in modern stoves is not really

RIGHT: *The Ekol Clarity double-sided wood-burning stove.*

glass but a type of ceramic. Don't be tempted to replace it with anything other than the correct material, as normal glass shatters from heat.

Convection

To further increase the convection element of a stove's heat output, some stoves have a second layer around their body with an air gap between and ventilation holes at the top and bottom. Air enters at the bottom, is warmed, loses density, rises, and comes out of holes at the top of the stove warmer than when it went in at the bottom. This flow of air helps to provide a more even heat distribution in the room.

Because of this extra 'skin', the sides of convection stoves are generally cooler than other stove types, which may be an advantage if you are worried about people, especially children, touching the sides of the stove. Some range-cooker stoves have convection sides, which allow you to build them into your kitchen units. If a stove has a convection top, be aware that it may not get hot enough to boil a kettle, and similarly a stove-top fan is also unlikely to get hot enough to work.

Inset and cassette

Inset and cassette stoves, designed to be installed within a wall, are becoming increasingly popular in the UK and offer a 'window of fire' effect. Cassette stoves, which were first invented (or at least named) by French stove manufacturer Fondis, have two boxes (like a convecting stove) around the fire, with air vents top and bottom to let the heated air into the room. Some models even have a built-in fan to increase the flow of warm air into the room. They take up less space than a free-standing stove – many can be installed in a wall slot approximately the same size as the stove. An inset or cassette stove installed in a plain wall offers a fairly minimal look and, if enhanced by an adjacent log store and a projecting hearth, can result in an impressive installation. Enclosing an inset or cassette fire with a fire surround and mantelpiece offers a traditional look with all the aesthetic benefits of an open fire, but much-improved efficiency.

Inset and cassette stove models are available purpose-designed to be built into an existing UK fireplace opening – a hole in a wall or a

RIGHT: *The Westfire 21 convection stove.*

new chimney breast. You can build the stove into a masonry wall or a new wall made from Thermalux sheets (which are self-supporting, insulating and, once sealed, can be directly plastered) or steel studding and fireboard. Although installation requirements vary from model to model, it is sometimes necessary to backfill any free space behind a cassette stove with suitable insulating material.

Inset stoves generally don't have the second layer of a cassette stove and so often need to be installed in a bigger chamber, which itself is ventilated at the top and bottom to recover heat to the room – and it is a good idea to make the high-level vents larger than those at the bottom to allow for the expansion of the heated air. This means more space is needed to install an inset stove than a cassette stove.

Some inset and cassette stoves are fitted with ready-made duct connections so that warmed air can be ducted to the same room or another room. Certain models aid the flow of warmed air using a fan-distribution system, which enables you to heat every room.

Range cookers

Range cookers are traditional in the UK. Initially, they were designed to burn coal, but there are now revised and modified designs for a wide choice of fuels, including logs. Range cookers are primarily designed for cooking, but will often be the only source of heat in a large kitchen.

Many Continental models were from the outset designed to burn logs and provide consistent and predictable oven temperatures, because the heat from the firebox circulates around the oven instead of just the two sides of some traditional designs.

Range-cooker stoves with integrated boilers combine cooking, heating and hot water. Some earlier cast-iron models, which take longer to heat up and give even oven temperatures, are designed to run all day. Other modern wood-burning ranges are of lighter construction, heat up relatively quickly and can be used intermittently.

Masonry and Kachelofens

For centuries, homes in Continental Europe (and in the last century

RIGHT: *The Fondis Ulys 900 double-sided inset stove allows allows you to see and use the fire from both sides.*

the United States) have been heated by mass masonry heaters and Kachelofens. Kachelofen is German for 'tiled stove' and these stoves are often covered in glazed tiles, giving them an ornate finish, or may be made from ceramic bricks detailed with coloured glazes, motifs and textures.

The principal purpose of these stoves is to have an occasional small fire, which is burned extremely hot and efficiently. The chimney pathways inside the stove are convoluted and encourage most of the heat to be absorbed by the large mass of stone from which the stove is made. This heat is slowly released into the room for many hours after the fire has gone out. The heat from a masonry stove isn't really controllable; once hot, it continues to provide heat for a long time, regardless of whether it is needed. Therefore masonry stoves aren't particularly well suited to a modern, well-insulated house, but do much better in an older house and/or one in a very cold place.

Silicon-carbide stoves are a modern take on the masonry stove. Again, heat is stored and slowly released over time, but silicon-carbide absorbs more heat than masonry, so the stove can be smaller. It also reflects heat very well, which results in an efficient burn, with high combustion temperatures in the firebox of up to 1,000°C.

Boiler

Boiler stoves can be connected to a heating and hot water system, and there are generally two types of boiler stove to choose from: clip-in and dedicated.

A clip-in boiler is small and retrofittable. It is usually a thin, rectangular metal box that replaces the firebrick at the back of the stove – take out the rear firebrick, knock out pre-cut holes to let the four tapping points on the boiler through the back of the stove, then fit the boiler in place of the firebrick. The heat from the fire passes into the water-filled clip-in boiler and then on to your heating and hot water system. Clip-in boilers cannot produce that much heat because the boiler takes up a fairly small proportion of the firebox and so absorbs a corresponding small amount of heat. A clip-in boiler will generally produce enough heat for your domestic hot water (the water you use for washing and bathing) and perhaps also a radiator.

LEFT: *The de Manincor wood-burning range stove with gas hob and electric oven.*

The Woodfire RX30 Panorama, a high output wood-burning insert boiler stove.

With a dedicated boiler stove the boiler actually forms the inside of the firebox, so the water in the boiler usually surrounds the fire at the sides, back and sometimes the top. This increases the surface area of the boiler and so increases the amount of heat transferred to water – sometimes enough heat for the whole house. Dedicated boiler stoves can be either free-standing or inset, and tend to give little heat to the room, passing most of it to water. This usually means it is a good idea to fit a radiator into the room where the stove is installed so you can make sure the room heats up quickly.

Technology has now progressed to the stage where some wood boiler stoves can even compete with the efficiency of an automated pellet stove. For example, the Walltherm Zebru achieves an efficiency of 93 per cent using the wood gasification technique, where the gases released from the burning wood are burned in a lower chamber at extremely high temperatures. Wood-gasification boilers are often confined to utility models installed in a shed or outbuilding, but Walltherm stoves are designed to be installed in the home.

The compact Klover Star 14 pellet boiler stove can provide central heating and hot water.

Pellet

Wood-pellet stoves are widespread on the Continent and increasingly popular in the UK. Wood pellets are made from sawdust forced through a press at high pressure, producing small, short, sausage-shaped pellets, usually 6mm or 8mm in diameter. The pellet surface is often slightly shiny due to the lignin in the wood, which melts at high temperatures in the press and binds the pellets together. Lignin, among other things, is the natural waterproofing agent found in the xylem – tissue that conducts water and minerals through trees.

Producing wood pellets requires more energy than producing the equivalent weight of logs, but still compares very well with fossil fuels and non-renewable electricity. Wood pellets have a low moisture content (typically around 8 per cent), contain more energy than the same volume of logs, and can be easily moved around by an auger (a spinning screw in a tube) because of their uniform size. Therefore pellet stoves can be fully automated like an oil or gas boiler, with a very consistent and efficient burn.

The pellets can be stored in a hopper in the stove itself (which is loaded manually) or be kept in a separate silo or hopper and fed to the pellet stove via an automated feed system. The separate hopper makes it possible to buy in bulk, which lowers the price and reduces the work of moving pellets around.

There are many wood-pellet boiler stoves, which provide hot water and space heating. Some have a window to the flames and are designed to be installed in the home; others are designed to be installed in an outbuilding or a garage. It is also possible to buy boilers with two fireboxes side by side – one for logs and one (automated) for pellets – which can be used separately or together. Wood-pellet inset stoves and cooking ranges are also available.

Pellet stoves are more complex than conventional wood-burning stoves, so it is important that whoever supplies and installs them is suitably experienced and qualified, not only to fit and commission them but to provide the necessary regular maintenance (*see* page 66).

Workshop

If you run a wood workshop, you might opt for a workshop stove. This allows you to heat your workshop and get rid of offcuts, which might otherwise be wasted, plus you can boil a kettle on it or cook some lunch.

Wood workshops often produce lots of sawdust and shavings. Sawdust extinguishes the fire in a normal stove, but some workshop stoves are designed to burn sawdust; others, such as the Oakfire range, can burn a mix of wood and sawdust. A word of caution: if you intend to burn shavings, be aware that they can burn very hot and fast, which can overheat the stove and chimney. This risk can be reduced if you mix the shavings with some sawdust, as it will dampen the fire. Filling a paper bag with your fuel and then compressing the air out is a safer way to reload a workshop stove that is already running.

You should avoid letting fine sawdust into the air, not only for the sake of your lungs but also because it can catch fire. An easy way to keep the area clear and tidy is to have a hearth which is higher than the workshop floor; and keep a guard around the stove so you don't accidentally lean lengths of wood against the stove or chimney.

LEFT: *Morsø 7943 – a contemporary Danish 7kW cylindrical wood-burning stove.*

Stove accessories

There are many accessories that can help to make your stove safe and easy to use. They also make great presents for stove enthusiasts.

Log baskets

Log baskets can be handy near the stove as a tidy store for kindling, newspaper and logs. There are many variations of the traditional wicker log basket and more modern ones made of metal or rubber.

Bellows

Although bellows may look the part, they are of little use with a stove, where the chimney and air vents do most of the work for you. Bellows come into their own with open fires.

Pokers or tongs

Pokers or tongs of some sort can be useful, but again, they are of more use with an open fire. They can be used to rearrange any errant logs that are already burning, or to poke ash through static grates.

Heatproof gloves

Heatproof gloves are definitely handy, and are often supplied with new stoves.

Stove-pipe thermometers

Stove-pipe thermometers can help keep the stove running optimally. The thermometer fixes to the first section of flue pipe coming off the stove and allows you to maintain the temperature of the flue pipe within the range at which the stove is running most efficiently. If the temperature dips too low or rises too high, you know you need to adjust the stove. Given time and experience, you'll probably come to know when the stove needs adjusting, but the thermometer is a good initial indicator, and is useful for guests or if you let a house with a stove.

Fire screens

Screens stop sparks flying out from the fire. They are of most use with an open fire or if you run the stove with the doors open .

Fire guards or nursery guards

Guards provide a safe zone around the stove so that people (in particular, babies and young children) cannot burn themselves. Guards are very useful for stoves in a public place, such as a bar or visitors centre, especially if the stove is near a thoroughfare.

Chopping blocks

You'll need a chopping block if you intend to make kindling by the stove. It should be dry, hard and fairly large – ideally a good 300mm or more in diameter. A round of oak does very nicely, especially if it's a knotty piece and therefore hard to split.

Hatchet

Next to the chopping block, or lodged in it like Excalibur, you'll have a hatchet for making kindling. Avoid choosing too small a hatchet or you'll need to strike the wood too hard to be accurate. Also ensure it isn't too sharp, so it is less likely to cut fingers and get stuck in a log.

Moisture meters

A moisture meter is useful to gauge the quality of a firewood delivery, and if it is near the stove you can test the logs as they go on and make sure they are ready to burn.

Moisture meters work on the principle that electricity flows better through a damp environment than a dry one. They have two sharp prongs that are inserted into the wood, after which a small current is passed through the log. The resistance or dryness is measured and converted into a reading. Different parts of the log give different readings, but a reading of over 25 per cent shows that the log needs to be stored for a longer period of time.

RIGHT: *A Charnwood Tor Pico wood-burning stove.*

Dustpans and brushes

A dustpan and brush makes sweeping up bits of wood, ash or bark a doddle. Often fireside toolsets also include a poker and tongs, though you are unlikely to need these for a stove.

Metal kettles

A metal kettle is useful for cups of tea; or, if you prefer coffee, buy a stove-top cafetière. Just ensure your stove doesn't have a convection top – it won't get hot enough for a kettle.

Metal buckets

If the stove has an ash pan, it's useful to have a metal bucket for emptying the ashes. The ashes can stay hot for hours after the stove has gone out and can safely cool off in the bucket.

Stove-top fans

Stove-top fans help spread the heat from a stove, especially if it's tucked into an alcove or a fireplace recess. These fans don't work well on a stove with a convection top, as it may not get hot enough to power the fan. There are two types of fan. The first uses a thermoelectric effect to convert a heat difference (in this case, the hot base of the fan sitting on the top of the stove and the cooler top of the fan) into electricity, which drives the fan motor. The second (our favourite) is a stove fan driven by a Stirling engine, which was invented by the Scotsman Robert Stirling in 1816. Its basic principle is that heat is used to expand a gas (air in this case), which pushes a piston upwards. Once the piston has risen, the air is cooled via heat transfer fins at the top of the fan and contracts, pulling the piston back down. When placed on top of the stove to warm for a while, the fan blade simply needs a little nudge and off it goes. This is possibly the ultimate stove boys' toy: you can watch the piston rise and fall, visible through the Pyrex glass piston cylinder.

RIGHT: *Aarrow i400F – A British made upright square multifuel stove with log store.*

CHAPTER THREE

Choosing a stove

66 *Whether you choose to buy your stove through a bricks-and-mortar shop or online, there are good and bad suppliers, so look for a company whose staff really know their stuff...* 99

LEFT: *A Contura 510 wood-burning stove.*

As well as looking the part, your stove needs to be up to the task. That very much depends on how much heat is needed and how you plan to use your stove. Install a stove that is too small and you are likely to become frustrated with it as well as having to burn it too hard; too large and you can end up overheating or running the stove too slowly, which is inefficient. In this chapter we give a few pointers on forward planning, explain how to choose the heat output needed, and take a quick look at those ever-important costs. Before you start, it makes sense to see if you can reduce the heat that is lost and wasted by your house in the first place. This may mean that you can choose a slightly smaller stove than you would otherwise have needed, and will certainly mean that you end up using less fuel, which is a year-on-year saving. We run through some of the things you might consider, many of which are not only very simple but also cost very little.

How do you intend to use your stove?

Most stoves in the UK are used to heat just one room, generally the living room. Usually central heating is already installed, so the stove is used to supplement the heat. You can also install a slightly larger stove and open the doors to let the heat spread to other rooms in the house – if you plan to do this tell your stove supplier, as you'll need to buy a larger model. Should you wish to go that bit further, a boiler stove will provide some or all of your hot water and heating.

Planning your heating system

Often a 'dry' (non-boiler) stove is installed in a room and provides heat to that room and perhaps adjacent rooms. The existing central heating system supplies heat and hot water throughout the rest of the house. While not as common as simply installing a dry stove into a living room, it is possible for the entire heating system to be run by just a 'wet' (boiler) stove. Or you may run a boiler stove in conjunction with an existing gas or oil boiler, providing all or some of the heating and hot water needed by the house. If you do choose a boiler stove, it's a good idea to make sure there is a radiator in the same room as the stove, to ensure the room heats up quickly.

RIGHT: *Aarrow Ecoburn Plus 5 – a traditional 5 kW steel-bodied multi-fuel stove.*

Wood-burning boiler stoves work well with many types of central heating systems, including radiators, underfloor heating, solar thermal heating and heat pumps. The design of any heating system, with or without a wood-burning stove, is a specialised business and we recommend that you talk to a qualified heating engineer who has experience in integrated systems.

Prepare your house – use less heat

Whether you would like to make your life more sustainable by using a renewable form of heating, or you just want to cut down on your fuel bills, it makes sense to look at how you can reduce your overall use of energy.

Insulate and draught-proof

Insulating your house will reduce the heat you need, so you'll use less fuel and save money. A house loses a lot of heat from the roof and walls, and through draughts and air changes. Insulating the roof is generally inexpensive and cost-effective. Replacing single-glazed windows with double- or triple-glazed windows further reduces energy consumption but may be relatively expensive. Even if you cannot afford to replace all your windows, some secondary glazing and heavier curtains help. Draught-proofing is fairly cheap, simple and effective.

There are government schemes and initiatives to help improve the energy efficiency of your home, details of which can be found on the Energy Saving Trust website (**www.energysavingrust.org.uk**). Some big energy providers are obliged to give something back, so they offer free improvements, such as loft or cavity wall insulation, if you qualify. Again, refer to the Energy Saving Trust to see if you meet the criteria and to find out which companies offer what.

Passivhaus design

If you are designing your own home or have more ambitious energy-saving plans, you might think about making your house a super-insulated Passivhaus – an energy performance standard developed in Germany in the early 1990s. The basic concept is to heavily insulate the house, have plenty of south-facing glazing to let sunshine do much of the heating, to maintain a high thermal mass

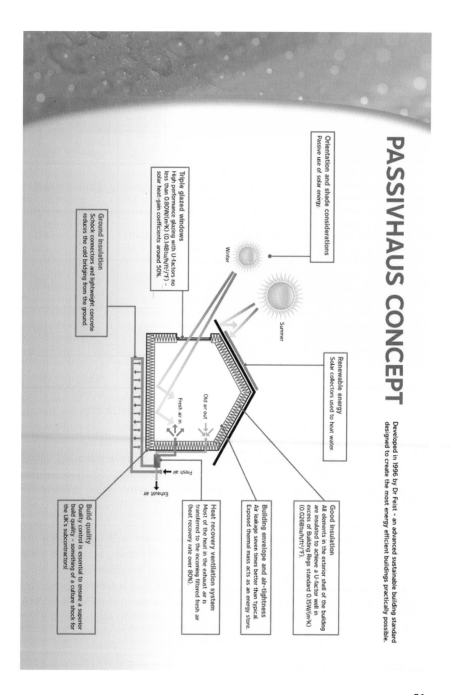

PASSIVHAUS CONCEPT

Developed in 1996 by Dr Feist - an advanced sustainable building standard designed to create the most energy efficient buildings practically possible.

Orientation and shade considerations
Passive use of solar energy.

Triple glazed windows
High performance glazing with U-factors no less than 0.80W/(m²K) (0.14Btu/h/ft²/°F) - solar heat-gain coefficients around 50%.

Ground insulation
Schöck connectors and lightweight concrete reduces the cold bridging from the ground.

Renewable energy
Solar collectors used to heat water.

Good insulation
All elements in the exterior shell of the building are insulated to achieve a U-factor well in excess of Building Regs standard 0.15W/(m²K) (0.026Btu/h/ft²/°F).

Building envelope and air-tightness
Air leakage seven times better than typical. Exposed thermal mass acts as an energy store.

Heat recovery ventilation system
Most of the heat in the exhaust air is transferred to the incoming filtered fresh air (heat recovery rate over 80%).

Build quality
Quality control is essential to ensure a superior build quality - something of a culture shock for the UK's subcontractors!

Winter

Summer

Fresh air in

Old air out

Fresh air

Exhaust air

Heat output from stoves needed for different types of housing and room volume

Room volume in m³ (length × width × height)	30	40	50	60	70	80
Uninsulated house	3.1kW	4.1kW	5.1kW	6.1kW	7.2kW	8.2kW
Uninsulated townhouse with a cavity wall	2.8kW	3.7kW	4.6kW	5.5kW	6.4kW	7.4kW
Renovated townhouse without a cavity wall	2.3kW	3.0kW	3.8kW	4.5kW	5.3kW	6.0kW
Renovated townhouse with a cavity wall	1.4kW	1.8kW	2.3kW	2.8kW	3.2kW	3.7kW
Modern house, post-2010	1.0kW	1.3kW	1.7kW	2.0kW	2.3kW	2.7kW
Passivhaus	0.4kW	0.5kW	0.6kW	0.8kW	0.9kW	1.0kW

to absorb heat, and to release the heat slowly back into the house, maintaining fairly even temperatures throughout.

The Passivhaus standard takes these principles and incorporates a heat recovery ventilation system, also known as 'mechanical ventilation with heat recovery' (MVHR), into the equation. Many of the heat losses in a house are to do with cold air getting in – either accidentally through unintended holes/gaps or through ventilation (trickle vents in windows, for example) that is needed to replenish fresh, oxygenated air supplies. Houses with MVHR systems are well sealed, with the central unit controlling the air entering and leaving the house. Heat from the warm air exiting is recovered and passed to the incoming air. The small cost of running the MVHR unit is far outweighed by the cost of the heat saved. However, one of the downsides of MVHR systems is that they rely on electrical power and do not function if the electric supply is interrupted.

RIGHT: *Esse 200XK DD – a traditional double-door British cast-iron 8.5kW multifuel stove.*

If you are interested in learning more about this approach to house design and refurbishment, look at *Green Building Magazine*, published by Green Building Press (see Resources). Its website (**www. greenbuildingmagazine.co.uk**) has a Green Building Forum, where members comment and discuss all aspects of green building.

Zoning

Most of the rooms in houses are used in different ways and at different times. Single-zone central heating systems heat every room in the house, whether or not this is necessary. In principle one can turn off individual radiators in rooms that need not be heated but this quickly becomes tedious. Being able to divide a house into zones that can be heated to different temperatures and at different times helps reduce the amount of energy used and is therefore economical.

The simplest way to zone your heating is probably to divide it into upstairs and downstairs, but you might want to separate bathrooms off into their own zone as well. Ask your heating engineer or plumber about zoning; it can be fairly cheap and simple to do, and saves money on your heating bill, regardless of whether or not you have a stove.

Sizing your stove

Stoves are rated according to their nominal heat output, which is measured in kilowatts (kW). This is usually, but not always, around 25 per cent less than the maximum output, so it's worth checking with your supplier. If a stove has a 5kW heat output it would be reasonable to assume a maximum output of around 6.5kW. When you size your stove, work to the nominal output and if in doubt, be a little generous. A stove that is slightly too big can easily be turned down, but if the stove is too small you will burn it flat-out, still not be warm enough and are likely to reduce its lifespan. If you choose a stove that is way too big it will only ever be able to run turned down, so it's unlikely to run efficiently and more likely to produce tar and blacken the window.

The table on page 52 shows what heat output is required. Remember that you need a higher output if you plan to allow heat to spread to other rooms in the house through open doors or hallways. If you live far to the north, high up or in an exposed position, you need to increase the results by up to 30 per cent. The physical size of the stove you choose depends on the available space (especially if you are installing it into a

Varde Aura1 – an example of DEFRA exempt stove.

fireplace opening) and how large your logs are. Generally the lowest-output stoves are 4–5kW; much smaller than that and you'd probably end up having to use twigs.

Heat load calculation

Your supplier should be able to perform an accurate heat load calculation for your room and/or house based on its size and the insulation values of the walls, floor, roof, windows, location and altitude. This is especially important when a heating and hot water system is being designed to be run by a boiler stove. You need to be sure that the stove is up to the job, but not too big, otherwise you will end up running it for long periods at a low output, which is inefficient and tends to block your chimney with soot. The way in which you plan to use your stove also has a bearing. If you light your stove for just a few hours in the evenings, rather than keeping it burning all day, you may need a stove with a higher output to counteract the fact that the walls will have cooled down between firings.

Buying a stove – how much will it cost?

There are lots of different products on the market, in showrooms and online. Many people visit a local showroom to look at the stoves, try the handles and controls in order to get a better idea of what is on the market.

When choosing a stove you might wish to consider whether:

- You want a wood or multi-fuel stove
- You want a contemporary or traditional design
- You want a large or small stove
- You want a large or small output
- Price matters
- There is a flue outlet size restriction for chimney.

You might also consider:

- How long the stove manufacturer has been around; a more established firm might have better designs, a proven track record and spare parts available.
- What the efficiency rating is
- Whether your supplier is steering you towards a particular model for the best reasons. It would be worth asking a few different suppliers to ensure you make a good choice

The directory at the back of the book lists UK stove manufacturers and distributors. The stove market is highly competitive and prices vary widely; as with many things, you generally get what you pay for.

Most manufacturers will be able to give you the names and addresses of good retailers in your area, and contacting one or more of them will be worthwhile. Experienced retailers promote manufacturers they know provide reliable products that are well supported with technical information and after-sales service. They will also recommend someone who can install your new stove.

When choosing your stove it is worth reading user reviews on **www. whatstove.co.uk**. Also, if you know anyone with a stove, ask what they think about it and if they had a positive experience with the supplier. Whether you choose to buy your stove through a bricks-and-

RIGHT: *Esse 525 DX – a contemporary British-made 5kW multi-fuel stove.*

mortar shop or online, there are good and bad suppliers, so look for a company whose staff really know their stuff and can lead you through the whole process.

You can spend anywhere between £350 and £2,000 on a new stove and £50 to £500 on a second-hand one. Boiler stoves, range cooker stoves and the 'show piece' contemporary stoves can end up costing over £7,000.

Inspect second-hand stoves thoroughly before purchase. If you decide to buy second-hand, choosing a well-known make at least offers you the opportunity to source genuine replacement parts and guidance on installation and servicing from the manufacturer.

Bear in mind that the chimney and installation can add up to as much as the stove or more. To install a stove is likely to cost anywhere between £200 and £1,500, depending on the size and complexity of the installation. Work out the prices first and you'll know what the final cost will be.

Smoke control areas

Check if you live in a smoke control area and which stoves you may be able to use by visiting the Defra website (**www.gov.uk/smoke-control-area-rules**). If you live in a smoke control area and have any doubts at all about what type of stove you can use and what types of fuel you can burn, contact the environmental health or building control department of your local authority for further information.

Defra exempt stoves have been tested and approved for use in smoke control areas because they have high efficiencies, low particulate emissions and the air supply to the fire cannot be completely shut off. Essentially this ensures the fire always carries on burning properly if there is fuel left to burn.

Overnight burning (or slow or slumber burning) is one of the least efficient ways to burn any fuel. Usually achieved by reducing the air supply to the fire, the resultant combustion is less complete than normal and can result in an increase of particulate emissions. Even if you don't live in a smoke control area, choose an efficient stove with low particulate emissions, as you will use less fuel and minimise your contribution to atmospheric pollution.

LEFT: *Westfire Uniq 23 Block Base – a traditionally shaped stove with a contemporary look and a wood-store stand.*

Installing a stove

❝ *However you choose to have your stove installed, it's up to you to ensure that the installation follows building regulations, the manufacturer's installation guide and any other legislation.* ❞

LEFT: *Firebelly FB2 wood-burner on log store.*

Having researched and chosen a stove, it's time to consider the more practical aspect of installation. Installing any new source of heat into your home requires effort and expense, and a stove is no different.

Who is going to install your stove? In most instances this is a choice between a registered competent person (in other words, a professional stove installer), a builder or yourself. We look at these options in more detail, highlighting what you should be aware of with each approach. In terms of costs, it's worth bearing in mind that the installation is likely to cost upwards of £200, and the materials for your chimney can cost more than the stove itself.

The chimney is the all-important 'engine' that drives the stove, so we explain the theory of how it works as well as the design principles that help ensure it functions as it should. Your stove and chimney will get hot, so it's vital that they are installed in a safe way to ensure that your home and family are not put at risk. The back-to-basics approach of looking at each part of a stove and chimney installation and thinking 'If this gets very hot, will something catch fire?' and 'Could smoke get out into the house?' is, in some ways, overly simple. But it's a good method, especially if you're trying to make certain that an installer has done a good job. We run through some of the stove and chimney regulations that are put in place to achieve a safe installation, and direct you to the relevant building regulations documentation, should you wish to read up in more detail.

Finally, for those taking the next step and installing a boiler stove, we discuss some of the more specialist requirements that these systems need.

Regulations and legal requirements

Various local and national regulations apply when installing a stove, and these relate mainly to the chimney and connections to the chimney. Below is an overview of regulations to consider. If a manufacturer specifies something in an installation manual that is more stringent than the building regulations, follow those instructions.

Dru 78 –11kW Dutch made traditional looking cast iron multi-fuel stove.

Smoke control areas

As mentioned in Chapter 3, first you should check if you live in a smoke control area by referring to Defra's website (**www.smoke control.defra.gov.uk**). If you live in a smoke control area, you need to choose a Defra exempt stove, which burns wood while keeping below a maximum level of particulate emissions in order to maintain air quality in densely populated places.

Conservation areas and listed buildings

Check if your local authority has any special requirements for chimneys before you start work. If you live in an area of outstanding natural beauty, a conservation area or have a listed building, there may also be restrictions on the type of chimney you can use; again, contact your local authority and/or the conservation officer. Sometimes a brick or brick-effect chimney stack is specified, or an external metal twin-wall flue pipe in a matt-black finish.

Building Regulations Document J

Stove and chimney installations come under your local authority and building control must be notified of the work. There are various building regulations to consider but Document J deals specifically with stoves and chimneys. You can download Document J from the government's Planning Portal website (**www.planningportal.gov.uk**). It is relatively straightforward and is designed to ensure that the stove works well and you don't burn your house down.

Most of the document deals with the chimney and flue pipe. An experienced stove installer should be familiar with the regulations that apply, which is another good reason for getting the stove installed by a professional.

CE testing

It is now a legal requirement for stoves to be CE tested and marked. Essentially this means that the stove has been tested to the relevant CE standard by an independent laboratory. The CE mark is a data plate giving various details of the stove and the standard to which it was tested. You should find it on the stove – it's usually fixed to the side or back, or it may be on a swing-out plate. A test certificate will also exist (usually as a PDF), which your supplier should be able to supply, should you wish to double-check.

Installer options

Most local authorities in England and Wales stipulate that you must either use a registered competent person, who will sign off the installation for you and register it with the local authority, or perform the installation under building regulations with inspections by a building control officer. Note that for boiler stoves, you must use a registered professional installer.

In the UK, stove installation courses usually last a few days. Compare this with Denmark, where even chimney-sweep training can take up to four years! Make sure that the stove installer you use, whether a competent person or not, is experienced and knows what they are doing. Good installers are usually booked up in the winter so it pays

LEFT: *An ACR Earlswood – a traditional 5kW multi-fuel stove.*

to plan ahead. Try and book in your installation in the summer; some installers even offer a lower rate for summer installations.

However you choose to have your stove installed, it's up to you to ensure that the installation follows building regulations, the manufacturer's installation guide and any other legislation. If you fail to do so and the installation isn't signed off properly, bear in mind that not only might it be unsafe, but also your house insurance policy is likely to be affected in the event of a fire.

Competent person installers

There are several competent-person schemes for stove installation, including schemes offered by HETAS, the Association of Plumbing and Heating Contractors (APHC) and the National Association for Professional Inspectors and Testers (NAPIT) – *see* Resources. HETAS focuses on stoves and has the greater coverage across the UK. Check the HETAS website (**www.hetas.co.uk**) to find an installer who is currently registered (with a membership number).

Installing under building control

Most local authority areas allow installations to take place under building control, so householders, builders or installers can do the work. A building regulations application form must be completed, giving a description of what is proposed and what materials are to be used. When the job is finished the installation is inspected and signed off by a building control officer.

Grants and other incentives

Reduced VAT on wood-burning stove installations

There are few grants available for log-burning stoves but there is a reduced rate of 5 per cent VAT for installing wood-burning boiler stoves. If you are installing a boiler stove that can burn only wood, or a wood-pellet boiler, and it is supplied and fitted by the same company, then the stove, flue, all the installation materials and the labour are chargeable at 5 per cent VAT. This can result in a considerable

RIGHT: *ACR Neo 3P – a 5kW multi-fuel pedestal stove with curved glass.*

saving and is an incentive to choose a wood-burning rather than a multi-fuel stove.

The Renewable Heat Incentive

The Renewable Heat Incentive (RHI) applies to the installation of pellet boilers certified by the Microgeneration Certificate Scheme (MCS; *see* Resources), log gasification boilers and wood-chip boilers. The starting rate for the Domestic RHI payments is 12.2p per kWh, paid for seven years, while commercial systems (in rented houses and businesses) are set at a lower level but will be paid for twenty years. Further information is available from the Energy Saving Trust website (**www.energysavingtrust.co.uk**) and the Ofgem website (**https://www.ofgem.gov.uk**).

Practical aspects of installation

When there are problems with a stove installation it is tempting to blame the stove, but most problems have nothing to do with the stove at all and are due to one or more of three key factors: chimney, ventilation or fuel. Classic symptoms such as smoke coming into the room, a very sluggish fire, blackening of the stove window, no heat given out or uncontrollability all suggest that one or a combination of these factors are in some way lacking, so it is essential to get it right to start with. We begin by looking at chimneys and ventilation before going on to look at other things that need to be considered when installing a stove. The subject of fuel is covered in Chapter 6.

Chimneys and flue pipes – theory and function

The chimney takes the flue gases, smoke and hot gases produced by the stove, and lets them out at a safe height outside. When a stove is hot and burning properly, you shouldn't see any visible smoke coming out of the chimney, unless perhaps you have just refuelled it. The chimney provides the draught to draw air into the firebox to ensure the wood burns well.

The temperature of the air in a house at the bottom of the chimney is usually higher than the temperature of the air outside at the top of the chimney. This means that the air at the bottom of the chimney is less dense than the air at the top, so air will tend to rise up the chimney. This temperature difference is vastly increased when the stove is lit – which is one of the reasons why a chimney often works better once the stove has been lit for a while, as the stove and chimney have both warmed up. The better insulated the chimney, the shorter the warm-up process.

Wind also increases the draw by creating an area of low pressure when it moves across the top of the chimney – this is known as the Venturi effect.

Below are general recommendations relating to height, bends and orientation of the chimney:

- Height – the chimney should be of sufficient height to create a good draw and get the flue gases clear of the house and any nearby windows.
- Termination height – the top of the chimney needs to be higher than the roof surface and not too close to nearby, taller structures, so that it is well out of wind eddies and turbulence found near roof surfaces, buildings, trees, and so on.
- Bends and orientation – the chimney should go straight up, wherever possible. Angled sections should be kept to a minimum, with no more than four bends in total. Bear in mind that if, for example, your house is in a valley with overhanging trees, you are more likely to have problems than if you are on a hilltop. In this case, installing a taller chimney would be likely to help. Building Regulations Document J gives many specifications you should follow, including minimum heights above your roof in different situations.

A common misconception is that a chimney needs bends in it to work properly. This is probably because many traditional masonry chimneys do bend because there was a fireplace on each floor of the house and each chimney had to bend away from the centre to make room for the one above. A bend in a chimney serving an open fire also stops rain entering the chimney and falling straight down into the grate.

Tar deposits

Another major consideration is tar deposits. Wood smoke has more tar than coal smoke and if the flue gases cool down too much as they

go up the chimney, the tars reach their 'dew point' (the temperature at which they solidify) and condense out of the smoke and onto the walls of the chimney. These tars can build up over time, reducing the internal area of the chimney; then it will not work well and will need to be swept. More significantly, these tars are highly flammable. If they catch fire, the resulting chimney fire can burn at extremely hot temperatures (over 1,200°C) and so is potentially life-threatening, as it can end up setting the rest of the house alight and might damage the chimney.

Reducing tar deposits helps reduce the risk of chimney fire and can be achieved by:

- Not burning wet wood (*see* Buying firewood, page 114)
- Not slumber burning (*see* Smoke control areas, page 59)
- Ensuring the chimney is insulated so that the gases don't cool too much
- Ensuring the internal diameter is not oversized, which helps the gases travel faster up the chimney, and not undersized so that it cannot quickly block
- Ensuring the internal surface of the chimney is smooth, giving a low surface area for deposits and a low resistance to the flow of the flue gases
- Choosing a chimney with a round cross section, as the flue gases move more slowly in the corners of square chimneys
- Using a pumice liner, as they are a lot warmer than clay or concrete liners, thus creating less soot
- Lining big and cold chimneys with a metal liner.

A chimney designed following these principles needs sweeping less often than a simple square brick chimney in a Victorian townhouse.

In the UK, chimney and flue pipe connections tend to be with the smaller (male) end downwards. An easy way to think of this is that if you poured water down from the top of the chimney, it should end up in the stove – or in the tee on the back of the stove if you use the rear exit.

LEFT: *Broseley Evolution 26 – a high output cast-iron boiler stove giving 16kW to water and 10kW to air.*

Lower flue gas temperatures of modern stoves

A modern, efficient wood-burning stove has relatively low flue gas temperatures (below 250°C when running) compared with older stoves and especially compared with open fires, where most of the heat goes up the chimney. This heat helps the chimney to draw and makes the design of the chimney for a modern wood-burning stove even more vital; let the temperature drop too low and the chimney will not draw well, meaning that the stove will not work well and the chimney will tend to soot up faster.

Sweeping access

It is very important to be able to sweep the chimney with ease, as a wood-burning stove should be swept at least once a year. It is usually possible to sweep through stoves, if the top flue exit has been used, by removing the baffle inside the stove. The resulting soot ends up back in the stove, where it can be removed. If the rear exit of the stove is used, a 90° or 135° tee is used so that the soot ends up in the dead leg of the tee, where it can be removed and where it cannot block the chimney or flue. If a stove cannot be swept through, an access door should be designed into the chimney.

Chimney and flue products

Now we move on to consider various different types of chimney and flue products available, and how they are used. This is by no means intended to be a comprehensive DIY guide to using these products. Refer to building regulations and/or have the installation carried out by an experienced installer. The regulations have not been included in this book, as they change over time and are too numerous to describe here.

Single-skin flue pipes

Single-skin flue pipes are often used to connect the stove to the chimney. This has the added benefit of passing a little more heat to

RIGHT: *Wallthem Zebru – a 93 per cent efficient gasifying boiler stove, giving 10.5kW to water and 4.5kW to air.*

the room, as it is uninsulated. But as previously explained, losing too much heat in this way isn't good for the functioning of the chimney, so the length of flue pipe should be kept within reason. We normally recommend not using more than 1,500mm of single-skin flue. Flue pipe is often thicker than flexible stainless steel chimney liner, and so is well suited as the first part of the chimney connected to the stove, which has to withstand the highest temperatures. Single-skin flue pipe can be cut to length as needed, and bends and adjustable lengths are available, making it easier to connect to a fixed chimney. The lengths are sealed using fire cement or high-temperature silicone.

If you are running single-skin flue pipe to connect to an insulated chimney coming through the ceiling above, make sure that you have to change over to the insulated chimney well below the ceiling height so that the ceiling doesn't get too hot. You need to change to double-skin flue at least 450mm below the ceiling to comply with building regulations. Single-skin flue pipe comes in various coloured enamel finishes; alternatively, if it is in stainless steel, it can be sprayed to match your stove.

Register plates

If you are installing a stove into an existing masonry chimney, whether you are using a flexible chimney liner or not, a register plate is used to seal off the chimney so that only the flue pipe goes up through it. The edges of the register plate are sealed to the chimney with mortar or fire cement so that the chimney draws only air through the stove. The register plate prevents any falling stones or debris from landing on top of the stove, into your room or onto you. It also holds the flexible chimney liner and retains insulating backfill such as Leca, stopping it from pouring out into the room. If no liner is used, or the chimney is large, the plate should have an access panel built in to allow for chimney sweeping. A register plate should be made of metal and can be custom-made by the better suppliers and installers.

If you don't use a liner, the flue pipe should protrude just a little above the plate – say, around 100mm. Many people mistakenly think that it should go as high as possible.

Chimney liners

Existing brick chimneys, or chimneys made with clay or concrete

Aga Ludlow – a 6kW cast-iron stove.

liners, often need to be relined and insulated in order to make them suitable for a modern wood-burning stove. An easy way to do this is to pull a continuous length of flexible stainless steel chimney liner down the chimney and surround it with insulation. The chimney liner has a round, smooth inner surface and ensures that no smoke can leak out (which can happen in old chimney stacks).

The liner must be pulled down or up the chimney, which is a two-person job – with one feeding the liner in from the coil while the other pulls on a rope attached to the liner. There are three types of insulation: Leca, rock-wool sleeves and an insulating wrap such as Linertherm. Leca is poured in to fill the space around the liner and chimney. Rock-wool sleeves are taped around the liner as it is installed. Linertherm is quite thin and looks like a fire blanket. It wraps around the liner and can be fitted through the chimney pot so there's no need to remove the pot. Some people use vermiculite backfill but it is not well suited, as it compresses if it gets damp, leaving the top part of the liner (where the flue gases are at their coolest and hence in most need of insulation) uninsulated.

Another way of lining an existing chimney is by using an insulating concrete-type product. A long balloon is pulled down the chimney, held off the sides so that it is central, inflated, and the bottom end sealed off. The insulating concrete-type material is poured down around the balloon and allowed to set, resulting in a smooth, insulated masonry chimney. This can also strengthen a chimney, filling in cracks and voids in the brick or stonework.

Twin-wall insulated chimney systems

A twin-wall insulated chimney system can be used to make a new chimney, usually in existing houses but also in new builds. It can be run either internally or externally, as required. An inner skin of stainless steel has an insulating layer around it (often 25mm thick) and an outer, weather-proof layer. The lengths twist, screw or push-fit together, with a locking band to hold them firmly in place. Various lengths, bends, elbows, tees, floor and wall-penetration components are available off-the-shelf, making this a relatively easy and quick product to install. Be sure to choose a type of twin-wall chimney where a closed-floor penetration component is available. Some types have a ventilated component, which could potentially spread smoke and fumes upstairs if there was a fire downstairs.

There's a wide range of roof flashings suited to most roof types – for example, slate, tile, flat roofs, corrugated roofs or polycarbonate. A good specialist company will also have solutions for specialist roofs such as sedum.

Most types of twin-wall chimney need a clearance of just 50mm to combustible materials (for example, floorboards), again making for a quick installation while not taking up too much valuable space in your house. It's worth checking this clearance, as not all are 50mm – the installation manual should clearly state this.

Internally you have to box in twin-wall chimneys if they are inside 'storage spaces', which includes bedrooms. This it to ensure that flammable items don't end up touching the chimney by accident. As well as the standard stainless finish, you can source powder-coated twin-wall chimney, usually in black, or in a colour of your choice at a premium.

LEFT: *Aduro 15 – a Danish 6.5kW oval wood-burning stove with curved glass.*

Pumice chimney systems

Pumice is manufactured from volcanic rock, and is ideal for making chimneys. Not only does it form a physically strong structure, it is also an inherently insulating material that can withstand the very high temperatures of a chimney fire, which most other types of chimney cannot. Pumice is a chimney system best suited to new builds or buildings undergoing major renovation. There are two main types: pumice liners, which are used inside a brick or block chimney stack, with the gap filled in with a Leca insulating backfill; and modular pumice chimney systems, which slot together (a bit like giant Lego) to form the finished stack all in one go. Some modular systems are a two-block system, with an inner and outer block, while others are single-block systems.

Modular-system materials are expensive but fast to install and economical with space, so can be more attractive than non-modular systems. Corbels suited to an externally rendered or a brick-clad stack are available with a chimney pot and finishing cap at the top.

Modular pumice systems are also well suited to timber frame buildings, as they can be installed freestanding on their own mini foundation, with stainless steel rods fixed into the foundation and held under tension at the top of the chimney for added strength and flexibility. Non-structural timbers can be run right up against the finished chimney.

Chimney pots

A chimney pot is a familiar sight in the UK. As well as adding a finishing touch to a masonry chimney, it also raises the chimney height. Chimney pots come in many shapes and sizes. One of the most common and simple is the roll-top, but there are a plethora of styles and colours to choose from. Have a look at houses in your local area and see which style is prevalent.

The pot is mortared on to the top of the chimney and the cement is flaunched so that the water runs off and away. Always use a water-proofer in a flaunching mix to prevent frost damage. A decorative fuel effect (DFE) chimney pot serves as both a chimney pot and cowl, and can be a practical way of simply finishing off your chimney.

Chimney cowls

The main function of a chimney cowl is to stop rain from getting inside the chimney. Rain not only cools the chimney down, which means the chimney takes longer warm up; it can also cause potential damage. Rainwater is slightly acidic and can eat away at your chimney, especially when combined with some of the acid products present in smoke. There are various styles of cowl, some of which are suited to more extreme weather conditions – ask your supplier for a recommendation.

The other function of a cowl is to stop or reduce downdraught – downdraught is when wind blows or gusts down the chimney, resulting in puffs of smoke coming out of the stove. There is a wide variety of anti-downdraught cowls to choose from. Fixed cowls, such as vedette or MAD cowls, require less maintenance and are better suited to stoves. Always ensure that the cowl can be swept through from below to avoid needing roof access. For this reason spinning cowls, while they can be effective, are generally not good with stoves. Stainless steel cowls are more expensive than steel cowls but they last a lot longer, as steel cowls are easily corroded, especially when burning coal.

Chimney fans

In extreme cases, where chimney draw is very poor and cannot be improved in any other way, a chimney fan can be used to suck the smoke out of the chimney. There are various sizes and types to suit most applications, but fans should be viewed as a last resort after other ways of improving the chimney draw have been tried. Fans can be placed externally on top of the chimney, or there are internal in-line versions.

Boilers and hot-water systems

A hot water tank allows you to store hot water for washing and bathing. Often a simple and effective setup is to have a boiler stove heat up the water tank first. Then, once the tank has reached a set temperature, transfer the heat to your radiators (or other form of heating). It's worth considering installing a solar-enabled hot water tank, even if you're not intending to install solar thermal straight away.

A solar thermal system is the perfect partner for a boiler stove, as the stove provides hot water and heating when the solar input is low; and the solar panels take over to provide hot water in the warmer months, when the stove isn't in use.

A thermal store is a large, well-insulated hot water tank. It makes it possible to store heat for use later – for example, you can programme your heating to come on in the morning before the stove is lit. By heating a large body of water you can also run your stove relatively fast (this is the most efficient and safe way of using a stove, especially a wood stove) without overheating your house, and you do not have to burn your stove all day to heat the whole house. A thermal store makes it easy to run your stove in conjunction with solar panels.

A remote tank thermometer is a great idea, as it allows you to monitor the temperature of the water in the thermal store and decide whether or not you should load up your stove.

Other considerations

Stove room ventilation

The fire needs a supply of air in order to be able to burn well, and when you open the door of your stove even more air is drawn through the stove and up the chimney. This means that air somehow needs to get into the room where your stove is. For low-output stoves, it may be that the existing ventilation in your house – such as window trickle vents, gaps under doors, and so on – is sufficient, but bear in mind that improvements such as fitting double glazing can reduce this ventilation. It can make sense to install dedicated ventilation even if you're not required to do so by regulations.

If you have extractors such as a cooker-hood extractor fan in a room connected to the room containing the stove, you will need to increase the ventilation to the room. Also consider providing a source of incoming air near the extractor so that it doesn't compete for air with the stove. Room ventilators are readily available and can be fitted with a core drill, making it a very simple part of the job.

In well-sealed modern houses, stoves that can draw all the air they need via an external air duct are increasingly used.

RIGHT: *Wanders Black Diamond – a Dutch-made wall-hung 8kW contemporary wood stove with three glass sides.*

Hearth

Stoves need to sit on a non-combustible hearth. If the floor is flammable, the hearth protects it from the heat given out by the stove and is where any falling sparks or embers land if the stove door is opened. The hearth also gives you a visible area around the stove to be kept clear of flammable items such as wood, carpets, chairs, and so on.

Minimum hearth sizes are given in Document J: essentially the minimum size of the hearth for a free-standing stove should be 840mm × 840mm, with at least 150mm to the sides of the stove and 300mm to the front. The stove manufacturer may specify something larger – if so, follow the instructions in the manual. If the stove will be used with the door sometimes open, consider increasing the distance to the front of the hearth. If you have an inset stove that is installed high up a wall, also consider increasing the distance that the hearth comes out to the front. Try dropping a small piece of wood from the position of the stove door a few times and see where it ends up.

Hearths are often made of masonry – for example, slate or brick – but off-the-shelf hearths made from toughened glass, resin or stone are also popular.

If the temperature under the stove has been tested and does not reach over 100°C a thin 12mm hearth can be used; if not, the hearth has to be a lot thicker.

The hearth and floor under the hearth needs to be able to take the weight of the stove. Most stoves are not all that heavy, but in some cases you may need to pay special attention to this.

Clearances and heat shielding

Stove and flue pipe can potentially get very hot: 300°C isn't uncommon for a flue pipe, and in the extreme case of a chimney fire this can rise to over 1,000°C, so make sure that any flammable objects around the stove and flue pipe are either far enough away or heat-shielded to protect them.

Most stove manufacturers state the minimum distances the stove should be from non-combustible and combustible materials, and you need to abide by these. Single-skin flue pipe has to be three times its diameter away from combustible materials – so a 150mm flue pipe needs to be at least 450mm away from something flammable. Often this is impossible, as the single-skin flue may have to run near a wooden lintel or mantelpiece, so heat-shielding may be required. Pay special attention to wooden lintels, curtains, skirting boards, wiring, plugs and furniture near the stove.

A good way of heat-shielding is to use 12mm fireboard with a 12mm air gap behind. The air gap can easily be achieved by cutting strips of the fireboard to use as spacers. Remember not to use metal fixings near the flue pipe, as these transfer heat through to the wood. As you can imagine, heat-shielding using just a thin piece of metal fixed directly to wood is not a very good solution.

Carbon monoxide alarms

It is a good idea, and a requirement under Document J, to install a carbon monoxide (CO) alarm. CO is a by-product of combustion and the more inefficient the combustion the more CO is produced. Under some circumstances it can be possible for this CO to leak into the house from the stove or flue pipe – another reason to install a stove in the correct way. CO is an odourless, tasteless gas, which can cause various effects, such as tiredness, headaches and flu-like symptoms. In extreme cases, it can make you pass out or worse. Wood smoke leaking into your house is less concerning than coal smoke, as wood smoke tends to make you cough and therefore alerts you to the problem, but you should still fit a CO alarm, whether burning wood or coal.

Fitting a CO alarm will alert you to raised CO levels. However, installing your stove safely, remembering to maintain your stove, flue pipe and chimney properly, and running your stove correctly are ways to stop CO becoming a problem in the first place.

Fireguards

A fireguard or nursery guard stops children from getting too close to a stove, and should always be installed where there are children under 12 in the house.

A children's playpen (the hexagonal type), folded out and fixed at the wall either side of the stove, makes a very effective and affordable nursery guard. The door section can be placed by the fire door to let you load the stove easily. They are usually covered in plastic and, if so, you need to make sure that they are far enough away from the stove – the correct distances from combustible materials (which this would be classed as) should be listed in the stove manual.

Load unit and flue thermostat

A load unit is essential for the serious boiler stove user. It pumps the water around the boiler in the stove and only when the water temperature has come up to above 60°C does it allow hot water out to the heating and hot water system and cool water back in. The high temperature is always maintained by the unit, which greatly improves heat output and efficiency, and reduces tar deposits and corrosion. The water tank only receives hot water from the stove, so the hot water reaching the tank is ready to use straight away.

A flue thermostat usually senses if the stove is running (when the flue pipe is hot) and switches the pump on.

High-temperature header tank

At the top of vented heating systems is a header tank that is open to the air. As the water in the system heats up, it expands and the level in the tanks rises, and vice versa. This header tank is also the last-ditch safety device into which steam can be vented in the event of the stove overheating, which is why the tank must be boil-proof and high temperature, as it can potentially get very hot. Most boiler stove installations in the UK are vented, although that is slowly changing.

In unvented systems, the system is sealed and the water expansion is taken up into an expansion vessel rather than a header tank. Most boiler stove installations in the EU are unvented.

Heat-leak devices

A heat-leak device takes heat away from the system if it is getting too hot, and at least one form of heat-leak device should be installed.

A heat-leak radiator is a radiator above the stove to which hot water can flow via thermo-syphoning. The hotter water from the stove (the 'flow') is less dense than the cooler water entering the stove (the 'return'), so the hotter water tends to rise up to the heat-leak radiator. Thermo-syphoning is essentially convection taking place in water.

To get this working correctly takes experience and can be tricky. A common practice is to use a large towel rail or large radiator in a bathroom as the heat-leak radiator, but this can be problematic, as the radiator can potentially get very hot and cannot be controlled. Ideally you should locate the heat-leak radiator in an unused space and control the water entering it with a valve and pipe thermostat, so it only comes on if there is overheating or a power failure.

Boiler stoves installed on unvented systems also have an overheat safety valve and coil fitted. If the water in the stove exceeds a certain temperature, mains cold water is flushed through the coil in the boiler, taking away heat, which is discharged as hot water.

As you can see, the system design and installation of a boiler stove is a lot more complicated than that of a dry stove and should be done by a registered competent person.

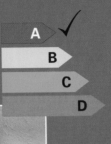

Using a stove

66 *There are many different
ways of lighting a stove,
and anyone who has
owned a stove for a
while has their
favoured technique.* 99

Even the best wood-burning stove needs your input to run well, and this is something you learn from experience. Every stove and installation is slightly different and will have its own character that you'll need to get used to. In this chapter we offer a few pointers to start you off in the right direction, from how to light a new stove for the first time, best practices for lighting and running your stove on a day-to-day basis, and regular maintenance and checks that you should be aware of.

At some point in your time together, you may find that your stove behaves a little oddly… Most common problems are actually nothing to do with the stove, so we run through a few simple things to look out for that will help you identify and solve these problems.

Lighting a new stove

When you light a stove for the first time, make sure all the windows are open, doors are closed, and leave the room empty for as long as possible. The paint, sealants and fire cement used in the stove and flue pipe cure at this stage, so you can expect a strange smell and sometimes a little smoke coming from the stove and/or flue pipe – this is completely normal. To begin with, light just a small fire for a short while and allow the stove to cool. The next fire can be a little hotter and last a while longer. Refer to the manufacturer's guidelines for exact guidance.

After the first few firings you can use the stove as normal, and it's important that you get the stove and flue hot for a good few hours to make sure that you cure the paint properly. Again, you may need to open the windows and close the doors until the paint has cured. Until this time, be aware that the paint will be more prone to scratching. All the above also holds true if you have just applied a fresh coat of paint to a stove.

There are many different ways of lighting a stove, and anyone who has owned a stove for a while has their favoured technique. Some methods can take time and effort – for example, where sheets of newspaper are twisted and shaped – which is fine if you have the time and inclination. But if the aim is merely to get the stove going, there are faster ways, and the method we propose here is simple yet effective.

RIGHT: *La Nordica Fortuna – an Italian steel and ceramic rotating cylindrical wood-burning stove.*

The theory of what you are doing is fairly straightforward: using paper and small pieces of wood, you light the fire and give it plenty of air. This initial phase is all about heating up the wood and the stove itself so you can use larger pieces of wood and start to get some heat into the room. When lighting a stove you need to pay attention to the fire and check it regularly – for example, it isn't a good idea to light the stove and get straight into the bath.

All the times given below are very approximate and depend on the type of wood you are using, the stove, the chimney and the weather. Lighting a stove is something you learn about and get a feel for through direct experience, a bit like swimming. This quick guide will get you started, but for real finesse trust your instincts and be guided by experience.

You will need kindling (*see* page 112) and paper. Newspaper is ideal (it doesn't matter which one – your stove isn't fussy or political). You could also try mixing in bits of cardboard – they can be useful, as they burn longer than paper. Firelighters work well too.

Before you light a fire, check inside the stove – has the ash build-up at the base become too thick? If so, take some away so there is space for your wood. There's no need to remove all the ash, as it forms a nice insulating bed for the fire, so only remove as much as you have to. But remember, if you're burning coal, you'll need to clear all the ash!

If your stove has a grate, make sure that the ash pan isn't too full. Take a small piece of kindling or a poker and dig a hole down through the ash to the grate so that there's a clear path for air to get to the base of the fire – this bottom supply of air is the 'turbo' for when you first light the fire.

Now follow these six steps:

1. Scrunch up five or six pieces of newspaper – not too tight or they won't burn well, not too loose or they'll burn too quickly. Put the balls of paper roughly in the middle of the firebox.
    Top Tip *If you have a sluggish chimney it will not draw well until it is warm (for long-term solutions, see 'Troubleshooting', page 100). Take a single piece of newspaper and scrunch it very lightly. Place it on top of the fire and light this sheet first. It will quickly burn and give the chimney a little burst of warmth, which can make the difference between a healthy fire and a firebox full of smoke.*

The six stages of lighting a stove

The Phoenix firelighter uses an advanced heating element to super-heat air.

2. Lay pieces of kindling over the top, a little like a boy-scout fire but it really doesn't have to be that neat. The idea is to allow air to get in and the flames need to be able to lick around each piece of wood as much as possible. Just laying the kindling flat on top of the paper in a bundle will smother the fire and won't allow the flames much access to the wood.
    Top Tip *Given the choice, use a softwood such as pine for kindling, as it burns hot and fast.*

3. Place a few larger pieces of wood on top of the kindling.
    Top Tip *Use medium-density wood such as ash or sycamore for the medium-sized logs that are put on next.*

4. Make sure that the air controls on the stove are open and light the newspaper. You probably need to light just one bit of the newspaper for the fire to take hold. Lots of people light several points at once, which is fine too. Some stoves light better with the ash pan door or main fire door opened a crack so the fire gets even more air. Your stove manual should mention this if it is the case, and ask your stove supplier if in doubt. If you do crack open

Checklist for safe and efficient wood-burning

- Only burn seasoned firewood (*see* The seasoning process, page 123).
- Stay with the stove while you are lighting it, until you have loaded it and turned it down to normal running temperature. Keep monitoring the stove while it is burning.
- Light the stove using dry kindling to heat up the firebox fast. You can use paper or firelighters to start the fire. Place the kindling in such a way that flames and air can get to as many parts of the kindling as possible. A pick-up-sticks pile is preferable to a bunched stack.
- The air vents should be fully open when first lighting the stove. You might also open the ash pan door or firebox door a crack. Refer to the manufacturer's guidelines.
- When the fire is going well, add a few bigger logs. When these are burning, shut down the air a little. If your stove has primary and secondary air controls, shut down the primary control and use the secondary air control.
- With all stoves – particularly modern, high-efficiency models – it is important to get the stove and chimney hot before you start turning it down. Turn the stove down too soon and the stove will smoke, blacken the glass and not burn properly.
- Do not slow or slumber-burn.
- Do not turn the stove down for the night.
- When the logs have burned down, but before they are reduced to embers and while there are still good flames in the firebox, add one or two more logs. You may need to increase the air supply a little to help the new logs catch fire, then decrease it once they are going well.
- When the stove is burning properly (other than when it is first lit or has just been refuelled), there should be no visible smoke coming out of the chimney – just a heat haze. If there is smoke, there is probably something wrong.
- Sweep your chimney at least once a year before the burning season. The frequency of sweeping depends on how much and what you burn.
- How often you should sweep the chimney is indicated by the amount of deposits that are produced at each sweeping. Frequent wood-burners should be swept at least twice a year. Consult an experienced chimney sweep if in doubt.

the door(s) it is even more important that you stay around until the stove is going well and shut the door(s).

5. The flames will spread through the paper and soon you should hear the crackle as the kindling starts to catch. Before long the kindling itself should be on fire, and the heat that this generates starts to take over from the paper. After about five minutes the kindling will be burning well and you can lay two or three medium-sized (50–75mm diameter) logs on top. Again, when you place the logs on the fire you should make sure you do not smother the fire and that air and flames can get through. Top Tip *Leave denser woods such as oak until the fire is well and truly going. Very large logs burn better split down; as a rule of thumb, try to keep their size down to under 150mm diameter. Also don't overfill your firebox.*

6. Once the logs have caught well (another four minutes or so) you can start to shut down the bottom air supply. Do it gradually, as suddenly shutting it can just kill the fire. If the fire goes from nice flames to smouldering and smoke, you know you've gone too far or too fast. The stove body should be starting to warm up at this point and you should feel heat coming out through the glass when you're in front of the stove. As a stove warms, there may be the occasional creak as the metal parts warm and expand.

Twenty minutes in and the fire is now properly established with hot embers building up at the base. If the primary air supply isn't yet totally shut, you should be able to close it at this point. Now regulate the fire using the secondary air supply, often found at the top of the stove. Some stoves have a simple combined air control lever – check your manual. The aim is to keep visible flames and no smoke. Before the logs totally disappear, add on another log or two. This gives the most efficient burn and the most consistent heat output. Top Tip *Pay attention to how your stove performs. If the chimney doesn't seem to be drawing as well as usual, this can be a sign that your flue or chimney needs sweeping.*

RIGHT: *Bruno T12 – a 21kW wood-burning convection stove with air tubes that blow warm air around the room.*

Troubleshooting

Symptom	Cause	Solution
Stove smokes into the room in puffs.	This is probably downdraught caused by wind blowing down the chimney. It only happens under certain wind conditions.	Insulate the chimney if you have not already done so; raise the height of the chimney; fit an anti-downdraught cowl.
Stove continually smokes into the room.	The chimney, flue or stove may be blocked. This may only happen under certain wind conditions. It may be caused by a lack of ventilation. To check this, open a window – does that solve the problem? Is there an extractor fan fitted in a room near the stove? This is a classic problem in pubs and restaurants. Turn it off and see if that solves the problem. It may be caused by a poor chimney – does it improve once the stove has been going for a while? In very rare cases this can be due to 'pressure difference' – when the air pressure in the room with the stove is lower than the pressure in another room or outside the house, which results in air being drawn down the chimney the wrong way. This generally only happens when there is wind.	Sweep the chimney and flue. Clean on top of the stove baffle. If opening the window solved the problem you probably need to fit a vent to the room, or check if an existing vent is blocked. If it improves after turning off an extractor fan, you need to install more ventilation to the room. Or fit a stove that can take its combustion air directly from outside. If it improves after the stove has been burning for a while, consider insulating your chimney if you have not done so already. You might also consider raising the chimney height a little. If the problem is pressure difference, the only solutions are to move the stove to another side of the house and another chimney if possible (which may work) or fit a flue fan.

Troubleshooting

Symptom	Cause	Solution
Stove gives out little heat; the window blackens up very fast. Stove needs to be burned flat-out or the fire dies.	It is likely that your wood is not well seasoned. Split a log and test the split face with a moisture meter (*see* page 116) – if it is above 25 per cent it is not well seasoned. Look at the end grain of the log – most species of well-seasoned wood have splits in the end grain. Smell the log – wet wood tends to have a characteristic smell that you can recognise over time. Try burning some kiln-dried wood or sawdust briquettes, which are guaranteed to be dry. Does that improve the performance? You may be simply burning the stove too slowly – you should have good visible flames, minimal smoke inside the firebox, and no visible smoke coming out of the chimney (just heat haze) when it is burning well.	Get a firewood moisture meter if you haven't already got one. If your fuel is not well seasoned, complain to your supplier if it was sold to you as seasoned. Consider sourcing your wood 1–2 years in advance and seasoning it yourself by stacking it well exposed to the wind but protected from direct rain. It should be cheaper to buy your wood unseasoned in bulk. Your stove supplier should be able to estimate your yearly consumption. Consider burning kiln-dried logs or sawdust briquettes – although initially a more expensive option, these can work out cheaper than burning badly seasoned wood, as you don't have to burn as much to get the same amount of heat. Follow the steps in the 'Checklist for safe and efficient wood-burning' *see* page 97.
Stove burns very fast, giving out little heat and is hard to turn down.	Check that the baffle is in place – if not, site it correctly or buy a new one if it has burned out. Check that you are using all the air controls on the stove correctly.	You may have a very strong chimney draw – consider fitting a flue damper to allow extra control over chimney draw.

Troubleshooting

Most problems with stove lighting and operation have nothing to do with the stove but are caused by a poor chimney, poor ventilation or poor fuel.

Although it is possible to give yourself the best chance of success by having your chimney designed by an expert, each installation is different and even the most perfectly designed chimney may not work in all locations or in all conditions. You can expect problems if it is a very still day with no wind and or a very warm, low-pressure day. You might also experience problems when there is lots of rainfall and strong winds.

The troubleshooting table on pages 100–101 sets out various problems, their causes and possible solutions. Before referring to the table it is a good idea to make sure that:

- the chimney is not blocked and has been swept
- the flue pipe connecting the stove to the chimney is not blocked and has been swept
- the area between the baffle plate and the flue exit has not been blocked by debris
- air can get into the firebox. Check that the ash pan is empty and the grate clear of ash to rule out potential problems (on a day-to-day basis, you would use a wood-burning stove with some ash in).

Stove maintenance

Sweeping and cleaning

The most important maintenance task for stoves is to sweep the chimney and flue pipe regularly (refer to the 'Checklist for safe and efficient wood-burning' on page 97). Also clean out the inside of the stove, including the baffle plate, behind it and the flue exit.

Ash removal

In most wood-burning stoves some ash can be allowed to build up on the grate (if the stove has one), as wood burns best with a supply of air

RIGHT: *The Woodfire CX12 wood-burning boiler stove, giving 9kW to water and 2kW to room.*

from above. Empty the ash pan (if there is one) before it is full, which helps to ensure there is always sufficient space between the grate and ash pan for air to get through. Remember that the ash may still be hot, so use a galvanised metal bucket, ash caddy or specialised vacuum cleaner attachments.

Summer ventilation

In the summer, when the stove is not in use, open the door a little to keep the stove and chimney well ventilated. This keeps the chimney drier and help prevent the stove from rusting.

Lighting a stove for the first time in the season

Before lighting the stove for the first time in the autumn, check that the chimney and flue are not blocked, as summer is a classic time for birds (especially jackdaws) to try and nest in your chimney – although ideally you should have a cowl with bird protection to avoid birds in the first place. Sweep the chimney before the start of the season. Check the baffle for damage, look behind the baffle and flue exit for blockages, and clear the ash from the grate and ash pan to check the grate for damage.

Cleaning the stove and covering minor scratches

If the stove has marks or dirt on the surface, when it is cold you can wipe it clean with a damp cloth. If there is a minor scratch, a quick spray with the right heat-resistant spray paint may do the trick. If the scratch mark is a little deeper, you may need to rub down the area with wire wool first before spraying. Remember to mask off areas such as the stove window and the surroundings, and ventilate the room well. Several light layers of paint are better than one thick layer. Don't use too much paint – if it is too thick, it might eventually peel off.

Some stoves are finished with graphite stove polish, although most modern stoves are finished with spray paint. If your stove has a polish finish, you can polish it every so often to keep it looking like new. A good way is to mix some stove polish with a solvent such as white spirit so it has the consistency of single cream, apply it evenly with a paint brush, allow it to dry for five to ten minutes and then buff it up with a large brush – a shoe brush or bath brush are ideal.

Cleaning the stove glass

Even with the most efficient airwash, it's likely that some tar or soot deposit will be left on the stove glass. Most of this gets burned off when the stove is running at maximum heat output. However, if the stove is left to die down at the end of an evening, by morning there will some soot on the glass. There are several ways of cleaning the stove glass:

Glass-cleaning pads

Glass cleaning pads are the quickest way to keep your glass looking as clean as the day your stove was installed. All that's needed is the pad itself, which can be stored close to your stove with the matches and kindling. No other newspaper, liquid or cloth is necessary. Just before you light the stove, rub the inside glass with the glass-cleaning pad and all deposits will be quickly removed. Don't worry – there's no chance that your glass will scratch.

Stove glass cleaners

There are various chemical stove glass cleaners on the market that are particularly good at removing badly stained glass. You'll need newspaper, protective gloves and paper towels or cleaning cloths, and your stove must be cold. Lay the newspaper below the stove door so that no glass cleaner marks the hearth. Either spray the liquid onto the inside of the glass or use a paper towel or cloth to wipe the dirty glass – avoid dripping the cleaner onto the metal body of the stove. Leave the product on the glass for the required time – approximately 20 minutes. Using a fresh paper towel, rub over the glass to remove tar residues. Keep wiping the glass until it is clean, finishing off with a clean paper towel or cloth to give a final polish.

Wood ash

Wood ash is a cheap and easy way to clean stove glass, but be aware that small, sharp particles in the ash could scratch the glass. You'll need a few sheets of clean newspaper and a bowl of water, and your stove should be cold. Crumple up a sheet of newspaper into a loose ball. Dip one side into the bowl of water, then dip the damp part of the paper into the wood ash in your stove. Now rub the glass with the newspaper. You'll find the wood ash acts as a gentle abrasive and removes any deposits. Use a fresh ball of damp newspaper for a final cleaning wipe of the glass.

CHAPTER SIX

Firewood and its sources

““ *Efforts are in place to encourage and increase wood supply, with a government target to increase supply by an extra two million tonnes of wood per year by 2020.* ””

The quality of your firewood is likely to be the one thing that has the most effect on how well your stove performs. You can choose the most efficient stove in the world and connect it to the perfect chimney, but it still won't work well or give out good heat if your wood is wet. Unfortunately, wet wood is still a common occurrence. A firewood supplier's idea of 'seasoned for a year' can in fact mean that the tree trunk has been lying around in their yard since February, they cut and chopped it on Monday and then delivered it to you on Tuesday.

In this chapter, we consider the benefits of wood as fuel and take a brief look at the structure of trees and how they grow before explaining the various forms of wood fuel, how to source firewood and how to quickly gauge its quality. We describe the burning properties of different woods and explain the importance of the seasoning process. Finally, we focus on how best to store and dry your firewood. Sourcing your own wood can be a great way to reduce costs if you have the space. We explain how to cut, split and store your wood so that it is dry and ready when needed. Indeed this holds true if you buy your wood; it may well need additional drying, and once dry, you need to ensure that it stays that way.

Wood as fuel

Wood is different from all other heating fuels. Gas and electricity are effectively 'piped' into your house, so once you have an agreement with the supplier you simply draw as much fuel as you want. Heating oil and coal are a little more like firewood in that you store them at home, check how much you have from time to time, and order new stocks when you are running low. An advantage of gas, electricity, oil and coal is that they are usually sourced from regulated companies. You can be fairly sure that the quality is good and you can easily compare prices by phone or on the Internet. This is not quite the case with firewood, although that is changing. Standards now exist, such as WoodSure (*see* Resources), which help ensure that an accredited supplier has wood of consistently good quality that meets minimum standards. Smaller firewood suppliers are learning to improve quality and launching websites, and bigger suppliers have also started to enter the fray. However, it is still vitally important to be able to tell just how good a load of firewood is, which we cover later in the chapter.

Wood is very tactile, and preparing and handling it can be an extremely enjoyable experience while also giving you a true feel for how much fuel you are burning. You can be justifiably proud of a lovely stack of firewood next to the stove in the living room. The same cannot be said of a full oil tank; try showing off about that to a visitor and they'd probably be nonplussed at best.

It could be argued that wood is the finest heating fuel of all. It is sustainable, often locally produced and competitive with other fuel costs, especially oil and liquid petroleum gas (LPG). It may become even more so as fossil fuel prices continue to rise. When your woodshed is full of seasoned wood ready to burn, concerns about Russian pipelines, road-haulage disputes and the influence of the Organisation of the Petroleum Exporting Countries (OPEC) are replaced by the security and comfort of having your own energy store. Firewood can also offer more than just security and control. Over time, as you get to know your suppliers and maybe gather some wood yourself, you can develop links with the countryside and the people who live and work there.

Our ancient wood-burning tradition was largely lost after the advent of first coal, then gas and oil. About a hundred years ago, woodland covered only 4 per cent of Britain. Now it covers around 12 per cent of the land, though this still compares with an average of 44 per cent for other parts of Europe (75 per cent for Sweden). This may help explain why the quality of wood fuel and our understanding of what constitutes proper firewood still need some improvement.

As fossil fuel reserves are diminishing and people are realising that they miss the cosiness, intimacy and general enjoyment that these other fuels can lack, we are starting to see the renaissance of wood. Efforts are in place to encourage and increase wood supply, with a government target to increase supply by an extra two million tonnes of wood per year by 2020. More information is available in the Forestry Commission's *A Woodfuel Strategy for England* (*see* Resources). In 1980, native species accounted for only five per cent of the trees planted in the UK. However, thanks to the efforts of conservation and organisations such as the Woodland Trust, this figure has risen to over 40 per cent.

Interestingly, the move to using more of our own firewood coincides with a strong movement towards awareness of where food comes and growing our own. Long-derelict allotments are once again thriving under the careful stewardship of a new generation of gardeners. People have much pleasure in growing food and the great sense of community that seems to accompany it. Firewood sits very comfortably with this general desire for more control of the food and fuel we bring into our homes. For some it offers a more sustainable and environmentally sound lifestyle, a chance to widen our network of friends and improve what is often called our 'social capital'.

Tree fundamentals

Despite their apparent simplicity, trees are surprisingly complex. Trees have four parts: roots, stem (or trunk), branches and leaves.

Roots provide the tree with a secure anchorage in the surrounding earth and supply the tree with most of the moisture and minerals that it needs to live and grow. While it's commonly believed that the roots of a tree are as large and expansive as its branches, this is mostly incorrect – look at any tree blown over by the wind and you'll see that the roots make up a relatively small part.

The tree trunk, or stem, has two functions: it elevates the plant to give its leaves the best opportunity to collect energy from the sun, and it acts as a store for the sugars created in the leaves and converted to starch. Branches form the intricate support network for the leaves, which themselves can take many forms, from the 'big flat plates' of sycamores to the 'needles' of conifers.

The leaves and bark covering the younger twigs of a tree contain chlorophyll, the powerhouse of virtually all plant life. Chlorophyll is critical to photosynthesis, the process by which green plants use energy from sunlight to convert carbon dioxide and water into glucose, releasing oxygen as a waste product. The tree grows by converting the glucose into building blocks for its cell walls – mainly cellulose, hemicellulose and lignin. When firewood is burned, this stored chemical energy from the sun is released as the chemicals quickly break down again.

If you look at the cross section of a freshly cut log (*see* opposite), it is possible to see how the tree has grown and the structure of the wood. The outer bark protects the tree, like a skin. Depending on the species of tree and the inherent dangers in that tree's natural environment, the outer bark can protect the tree from fire and physical damage in addition to providing a waterproof skin.

Between the outer bark and the inner wood is a very thin layer of living cells called the cambium, which each year grows into a new layer of wood and thickens the bark. In some species these 'annual rings' are

Growth rings

Pith

Sapwood

Heartwood

Cambium

Bark

fairly obvious and the tree's age can be determined by counting them. This is easiest to do with oak, ash, elm and sweet chestnut. The dark and light annual rings are not, as some believe, winter and summer but spring and summer wood. The lighter part of the annual ring is the rapidly grown spring wood, while the darker part is the slower-growing summer wood.

The wood itself is made up of two parts – sapwood and heartwood. Sapwood is usually light in colour and is a mass of tiny pipes (the xylem), through which water flows up the tree from the roots. Heartwood is dead and darker in colour, as all the pipes are blocked up (mainly by lignin). Heartwood serves to strengthen the tree but a tree can survive quite easily without it, as evidenced by the many hollow trees that exist.

Types of wood fuel

Wood fuel comes in several different forms, the most common being logs. But there are also wood pellets, wood chips, manufactured logs and kindling.

Logs

Logs are the simplest form of wood fuel, comprising the trunk and branches cross-cut into short lengths (usually 200–300mm long). It is important to know the maximum log length that your wood-burning stove can take, and buy or cut your wood accordingly. However, it's easier to make and maintain a good fire with various log sizes, so always try to ensure your woodshed has a good mixture available for burning.

Kindling

The ancient word 'kindling' describes the little sticks used to start a fire. Kindling can simply be small, dry sticks gathered from a hedgerow, or wood chopped into small pieces of roughly 25mm diameter. Knot-free conifer logs make excellent kindling, with pine among the most popular species. Bark and pine cones can also be used to good effect.

Wood pellets

Pellet stoves are viable replacements for oil or gas burners and are gaining in popularity. They use a reconstituted wood fuel made from either pulverised wood or wood waste extruded into small pellets. Pellets are clean, easy to move around and have a relatively low moisture content. Choose DIN-plus-rated pellets, as these adhere to clear minimum standards – for example, they have a moisture content of ten per cent or less. Store the pellets in a dry space.

Wood briquettes

Made by the same process as wood pellets, briquettes are extruded into cylinders around 50–75mm in diameter and 150–300mm long. With a moisture level of around 8–10 per cent, briquettes provide a lot of heat per kilogram. It can be handy to have a bag of briquettes for times when you have run out of wood or the fire needs a little boost.

Wood chips

These are less heavily processed than wood pellets and are best suited to larger automated wood boilers of the type used to heat very large homes, schools, hospitals and, at the industrial level, wood-fuelled power stations. Wood chips are hugely important as we move towards using wood as a source of renewable energy, but are of very limited interest to the owner of a modern wood-burning stove.

Buying firewood

In many ways, buying firewood is the single most important part of owning a wood-burning stove. Getting this right will ensure that your stove is a source of comfort and pleasure; getting it wrong can make your life a nightmare!

Although buying wood fuel is different from buying electricity, gas, oil and coal, there are now a number of recognised wood-fuel-quality schemes. These accredited producers or suppliers have to demonstrate compliance with recognised quality standards, which also consider the source and sustainability of the wood products they sell.

The organisation WoodSure ensures that the wood sold by its suppliers meets a certain fuel quality – all members are checked annually. You can find WoodSure-accredited suppliers via their website (www.woodsure.co.uk). HETAS runs an accreditation scheme that works in much the same way. It publishes an annual guide of approved products and services, and the guide and HETAS website include a directory of accredited producers and suppliers (*see* Resources).

As a general rule, it's usual to buy your wood by volume rather than weight. The volume of wood varies very little as it dries but its weight varies hugely, as freshly cut logs usually contain at least 50 per cent water. If you choose to buy logs by weight, it's important that you get some assurance or guarantee of their moisture content. With the growing interest in wood burning, specialised suppliers have entered the market, and several offer logs that have been kiln-dried to reduce their moisture content. If you buy dried logs, you will know how much energy you are buying; just as importantly, your wood fuel is immediately ready to use.

Wood can be bought in various ways, including from the back of a truck or trailer, in pre-packed bags, in dumpy bags or as pallet stacks of kiln-dried timber. However you choose to buy it, we recommend that you shop around to ensure the wood is of good quality. It's a good idea to make the seller aware of your investment in a wood-burning stove and that you will be buying firewood for many years. Building a relationship with a firewood supplier is key to ensuring a regular, reliable source of quality firewood. Merchants can be sourced via the usual channels – adverts in the local paper or on the Internet – but don't forget to ask for recommendations from those who are already burning logs. For even greater peace of mind, try and visit your intended supplier to see how the wood is handled, cut and seasoned. Buying a whole year's supply of freshly felled wood and seasoning it yourself can save money, as wet wood and bigger loads should be cheaper, but you'll need space for the current year's supply and the year's supply that is drying.

We look at seasoning in more detail later in the chapter (*see* page 123), but for now it's important to know whether the wood is freshly cut or has been seasoned – and if so, for how long. With experience you'll learn to observe and smell logs and instantly judge how well seasoned they are. Good signs to watch for include:

- The bark is cracking and falling off.
- There are radial cracks on the cut ends.
- The logs make a high pitch when hit instead of a dull thud.

- Wood has turned grey if it has been exposed to sunlight for a long time.
- The logs feel light and smell dry.
- Logs are easy to ignite and don't hiss too much when burning.
- A log split in half has a moisture content of 25 per cent or lower when a moisture reading is taken off the freshly split face.

A fun way of testing the wood requires washing-up liquid and a good set of lungs. Wipe a layer of washing-up liquid onto one end of a log and then blow down the other end. Well-seasoned wood produces several bubbles and foam; wet wood is hard to blow down and hardly produce any bubbles at all.

Freshly cut wood usually has around 40–50 per cent moisture content, which should be brought down to 25 per cent with kiln-drying or air-drying (seasoning). To take an accurate moisture reading, use a moisture meter to measure the moisture on the inside of a piece of firewood; the firewood is drier on the outside where the wind and sun has got to it. Split a chunk of firewood down the middle, push the two pins on the end of the moisture meter into one of the freshly split faces (not the end grain or outside faces), ideally near where the middle of the piece was before you split it, and turn on the meter. The reading will appear on the screen as a percentage.

Finally, be sure to discuss delivery with the supplier. How far will they deliver? Is delivery free? If not, what is the charge? When and how will the supplier deliver – will they simply tip the logs in your drive or take them your woodshed?

Bags of firewood logs are commonly sold in garage forecourts, but only consider buying this wood if it is clearly branded and from a known and reliable supplier. Often the wood is from unseasoned conifer, which burns poorly, can be very expensive, and may not be good for the life of your stove or chimney.

Gathering firewood

It may seem obvious but you can't just pick up wood you see in woodlands or beside the road without asking the owner first. A small pile of logs where there has been work on overhanging trees may sit there for weeks, but it still belongs to someone. In Britain we have the common right to gather wild food for individual use, but this right doesn't extend to wood fuel. The exception to this rule is the rare case where an ancient right to gather fuel wood exists and applies to an individual property, a group of houses or sometimes an entire village.

In recent years there has been an increased interest in people wanting to own a small woodland. These woodlands come on to the market only occasionally and nowadays command a high price per acre – further information is available from the Small Woods Association and the Royal Forestry Society (*see* Resources). Owning your own woodland is the ultimate solution to the need for a permanent wood supply, but there are still certain rules governing aspects of management and how much wood you can cut each year. The critical question for those who already own woodland, or are thinking of buying a patch, is how much you need to enable you to sustainably harvest enough firewood to keep your home warm. A very broad rule of thumb is that broadleaved woodland grows about 3–4m^3 of wood per hectare per year. There is a huge variation in woodland productivity, depending on the tree species involved, the soil type, rainfall and altitude. It used to be said that if a farmer had 20 acres of woodland, he could keep his farmhouse warm all year (a hectare is 2.47 acres).

As the owner of a wood-burning stove, you will quickly develop an eye for every twig, branch or scrap piece of wood that you think you can burn. While scrap wood is seldom enough to meet your annual needs, it can make a contribution. Don't be surprised to find yourself looking in skips to see how much wood someone has thrown away (but do remember not to burn treated or painted wood). If you see a tree surgeon at work, ask him what he is going to do with the logs or branch wood. Also remind your neighbours of your interest in wood if they might be able to supply any.

Burning recovered or scrap wood

Having mentioned the amount of wood that is wasted each year, it is only right to consider a few points of caution before you consider collecting and burning it.

Scrap wood may well contain old nails, screws and possibly shards of glass if the wood has come from window frames. Avoid burning painted or treated wood. Some of the insecticides used in the past were highly toxic and included organochlorines (chemicals that contain carbon and chlorine). Fungicides also contained highly toxic chemicals such as arsenic. Although these toxic components become stable salts when used in wood treatment, they may become unstable when roasted in a fire. Wood treated with creosote, wood tar or some of the earlier wood preservatives is usually more flammable than natural wood and can burn out of control in a stove. If you burn treated wood, the ash may also be contaminated. Ash can otherwise be useful in the garden – to enrich compost, discourage slugs and snails, and lay paths. Wooden pallets can be burned, as they are generally untreated, but plywood, medium-density fibreboard (MDF), oriented strand board (OSB) and other manufactured woods should not be burned either.

If you are at all uncertain whether scrap wood is safe to burn then the simple rule is don't use it!

The best woods to burn

Hardwood vs softwood

Hardwoods come from broadleaved, deciduous trees – the main ones being ash, beech, birch, cherry, elm, sycamore, chestnut and oak. Softwoods come from coniferous trees, which are usually evergreen with needle-like leaves, such as cedar, fir and pine. There are exceptions: larch is a deciduous softwood, for example. Hardwoods tend to have a lower moisture content when felled and are generally denser than softwoods so will occupy less space.

If you buy your wood by volume, which is very likely, certain types of wood are much better value than others. For example, larch, which makes fine firewood and excellent kindling, is around 30 per cent less dense than oak. Therefore it should be worth 30 per cent less by volume if it has the same moisture content. The other thing to consider is that the denser the fuel, the less space it takes in your woodshed, the less wood you have to carry around and the longer the logs will burn.

Softwoods make excellent kindling, as they catch fire easily and burn fast and hot. If you have a range cooker stove and want to boost the oven or do some stir-frying, a load of small softwood soon gets everything nice and hot. But if you want to leave the stove running for a long time, use dense hardwood such as oak.

The ancient rhyme on pages 120–21 recommends the best woods for open fires. However most of its suggestions should be taken with a pinch of salt – especially the claims about elm and ash!

Types of wood

Alder

A large tree with a conical crown and glossy dark green leaves, alder is most commonly found on wet ground and by streams and rivers. It grows quickly and burns well, and is also very easy to split; the freshly cut wood is white but soon turns dark orange, which readily identifies alder among other logs.

Ash

Tall and graceful, ash has pale brown-grey bark and pinnate light green leaves. Freshly cut ash has a low moisture content and so seasons fast, which is why it is so often hailed as a great firewood. Once seasoned, ash makes fine, but not exceptional, firewood. Burning ash green is a bad idea. It may burn but it's still a very poor fuel.

Beech

Beech is a large deciduous tree with smooth grey bark and a broad, spreading crown. Wood from this shady tree is best known for fine furniture and flooring, and provides first-class firewood. Beech firewood mostly comes from thinnings or as branch wood from felled mature trees. However it does not coppice very well.

Birch

Some say the graceful silver birch is our most beautiful tree, which is why it is often called 'the lady of the woods'. It makes excellent firewood and is the primary fuel in many parts of northern Europe. Birch splits well but is apt to rot very quickly so take extra care during seasoning. Its smoke is particularly aromatic.

Beechwood fires are bright and clear,

If the logs are kept a year.

Chestnut's only good, they say,

If for long it's laid away.

Birch and fir logs burn too fast,

Blaze up bright and do not last.

Elm wood burns like a churchyard mould,

Even the very flames are cold.

Poplar gives a bitter smoke,

Fills your eyes and makes you choke.

Apple wood will scent your room

With an incense-like perfume.

Oak and maple, if dry and old,

Keep away the winter cold.

But ash wood wet and ash wood dry,

A king shall warm his slippers by.

Oak

Oaks are sturdy with a broad crown and silvery-brown bark that becomes rugged with age. As a general rule, freshly cut oak firewood should be seasoned for two years, as it is very slow to dry. For a shorter seasoning period, the logs should be split into small pieces – say, 8cm in diameter – which can be ready to burn after one summer.

Sycamore

A member of the maple family, sycamore is strong in the face of winter gales and provides welcome shade on hot summer days, but each spring it acts as a host to millions of aphids when the leaves produce a mass of honeydew. Sycamore is easy to chop when wet but has a tendency to break off into chunks when dry.

Larch

Larch and Douglas fir plantations were encouraged in the past so they are now a fairly common sight. However, due to the spread of *Phytophthora* fungus, many larch trees in Britain are being felled. Larch is a deciduous conifer with needle-like light green leaves. It burns hot and fast and makes excellent kindling; you can also burn larger logs.

Douglas fir

An evergreen conifer native to the United States, Douglas fir was introduced to the UK in 1827 by Scottish botanist David Douglas. It thrives in western areas of the UK, where rainfall is highest, and is widely used as a constructional timber and for cladding. The wood is stable and not too sappy with a reddish colour. It burns well, but fast.

Thorn and fruit tree wood

Although perhaps hard to get hold of, thorn and fruit tree firewood is the best of all. Hawthorn, apple and pear all burn well, giving excellent embers and a wonderfully scented wood smoke. Hawthorn will even burn well when still 'green' but nonetheless should be seasoned first. Logs to lay aside for Christmas perhaps.

Willow and poplar

These trees are widespread and fast-growing but make poor firewood. The wood burns in a wood stove but it's advisable to burn it with better-burning woods. The small withies from coppiced willow make excellent kindling without chopping, but willow does spit so make sure you close the stove door.

The seasoning process

Countrymen can talk and argue for hours about the seasoning of firewood, the needs of each species, and whether or not to split the wood. How many years does it take for oak to season? Can you burn pine?

'Seasoning' simply means the initial drying of logs. And, unlike cheese and wine, logs do not improve by ageing. In fact, keep the logs for too long and they start to lose their heat value as they are broken down by fungi. This drying process is complicated by the structure of the wood and bark, and by the fact that we are not simply removing water. Tree sap always contains a wide range of dissolved mineral salts, and in certain species and at certain times of year the sap may have a high content of sugars. These compounds are hygroscopic (they absorb water), which to some extent makes drying firewood a little like trying to dry a towel that is wet with sea water; the fluids within coniferous timber are even more complicated. Only once logs have dried to around 25 per cent moisture or less do they merit being called firewood.

Before wood can burn, the water it contains needs to be heated up and turned to steam so that it evaporates. This takes a lot of energy, and that energy comes from the fire – energy that would otherwise be given to your room as heat. The heat from firewood is measured in kilowatt hours (kWh). The wetter the wood the less kWh you get out of it, so if you bought your firewood this makes the heat you actually get from it increasingly expensive. So although a reliable supplier who delivers well-seasoned wood may charge a little more, it may work out better value in the long run.

Some firewood suppliers claim that the wood they supply is seasoned when it is not. The first you know of it may well be when you notice that your wood-burning stove is hard to light, is giving out less heat, is harder to control and the window is getting tarred up. It doesn't just stop there: burning unseasoned wood tars up your chimney (increasing the risk of a chimney fire) and reduces the life of your stove and chimney. Burning unseasoned wood is inefficient and results in high levels of particulates, which is bad for health. The moisture content of your firewood is probably the single most important factor in getting heat out of your stove, which is why a firewood moisture meter can be so important.

The following graph shows how the moisture content of the wood affects the heat output of the stove.

Energy content in firewood at different moisture contents

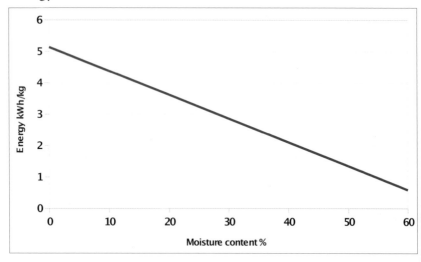

Trying to light a fire with damp wood is not only frustrating but also smoky and smelly. Once the fire is lit, it will be slow to get going and give out little heat, even though you give it plenty of air. After a while the wood will dry out and the stove can suddenly become too hot for a short period as the wood burns out.

Soot and tar on glass is annoying but can be easily remedied (*see* page 105); what happens in the chimney is more serious. Tar build-up is what causes chimney fires. The tar itself is flammable and can accumulate inside the chimney to the point at which it catches fire. It roars away and will get extremely hot – from 1,000 to 1,200°C. This can damage the chimney and could eventually set fire to the house.

The build-up of tar and soot in the chimney reduces the size of the flueway, which can cause your stove to smoke, and could ultimately block it completely. Not only does smoke make an unpleasant smell but also the carbon monoxide it contains is bad for your health. You will have a carbon monoxide alarm fitted already, which will alert you to something being wrong, but it is best to avoid such a situation.

There are a few tree species that people swear you can burn 'green' (freshly cut and unseasoned), the best example being freshly cut ash. This is because freshly cut ash tends to have a lower moisture content than other woods – around 33 per cent moisture instead of 40–50 per cent plus. While it is physically possible to burn freshly cut ash (as is possible for many types of wood at 33 per cent moisture), it would be unwise to do so for the reasons outlined above.

If you are convinced by the advantages of seasoning, the next thing to consider is how to handle your wood logs. We look at the pre-storage preparation of the logs themselves before moving on to basic woodshed design.

Preparing logs for storage

Wood loses water best through the cut ends of a log, and after that through any split surfaces. So if you have tree trunks or big branches, the first step is to cut them into rounds of the right length for your stove. Once cut, the drying is considerably improved by splitting the log before storing it in the woodshed, as the bark-encased sides are largely waterproof. So, for the quickest and most effective seasoning, any log with a diameter greater than 100mm should be split before storing.

The length of time it takes to season the logs varies, depending on

the tree species, the size of the logs and which part of Britain you live in. Oak needs two years or more of seasoning. Traditional saw millers cutting oak planks and beams advised to allow a year of air-drying for every 25mm of thickness, although they were as much concerned with splitting and warping as the actual drying.

With the exception of oak, almost all other hardwood or broad-leaved trees (beeches, birches, maples, and so on) can be grouped together under the general advice of cutting this winter for burning next winter. The logs are best harvested when the trees are dormant and contain relatively little sap, and they then have the entire spring, summer and autumn to dry out.

You may live in an area where there is an abundance of conifer forest and a proportion of your firewood may come from these conifers. Softwood or coniferous trees include pines, firs, spruces, larches, hemlocks and cedars. Some conifers such as pine can be particularly resinous and may need longer seasoning.

Some people advise using conifer as little as possible and buying broadleaved firewood instead, but we must bear in mind that in much of Scandinavia, conifer firewood is the norm.

Splitting logs

There are three ways to split a log: use a simple old-fashioned axe, a sledgehammer and wedges, or a hydraulic ram.

Splitting axe

Let's start with a splitting axe (including the splitting mauls specifically designed for difficult logs). If you are going to use an axe, it should have a good strong handle, be heavy enough (say, 1.8kg or more) and, ironically, be relatively blunt – when splitting wood with a sharp axe it can frequently jam without splitting the log.

Practise hitting the same spot time after time and you will settle into a rhythmic pattern of log splitting. Work at a steady pace and let the axe do the work rather than putting too much force into the blow. In this way you may be able to work for several hours without really tiring and split a large stack of wood. Stay safe by keeping the area you are standing in clear of split wood, and don't let anybody who is watching or helping come anywhere near you while you are splitting. Occasionally you will misjudge a log and the axe may ricochet with the risk of injury to anyone close. Also resist the temptation to wear gloves when working with an axe. You need a good grip and to feel the axe shaft; wearing gloves inhibits this and makes your work clumsier. If possible don't work in the rain when the axe handle and logs are wet. Everything just gets slippery and you are much more likely to have an accident.

Choose your chopping block carefully. You need a fairly large, tough log on which to split all your other firewood logs. The best chopping blocks are made from the lowest part of the tree trunk (the stump), the very first part of the tree that is above ground. A chopping block made from a tree stump almost always has some buttressing where it widens out in contact with the roots, and the wood fibres are matted, making it much more difficult to split. Some people recommend placing the chopping block inside an old car tyre. This contains the pieces of wood you are splitting, so less time and effort is required seeking and collecting errant pieces. It may seem obvious but don't try to split large logs in half straight away – you are liable to get the axe stuck! Instead, work around the edge of the log, splitting off smaller segments, and look out for existing splits you can take advantage of.

Sledgehammer and wedges

The basic skills required when using sledgehammer and wedges are very similar to those needed for axe work. You probably still have a chopping block, and your swing with the sledgehammer needs to be accurate enough to hit the wedge cleanly. You can buy wedges that are specifically designed for splitting firewood logs – they are round or star-shaped cones. A word of caution though: hitting an iron or steel wedge with an iron sledgehammer is dangerous, as tiny splinters of iron can fly out like pieces of shrapnel. To minimise the risk of eye injury, wear protective goggles and use wedges made of nylon or a soft magnesium alloy, which don't splinter.

Hydraulic ram systems

If you don't want to use an axe or a sledgehammer, or you expect to be working with large knotty logs that are hard to split, you should consider one of the many hydraulic ram systems that are currently on the market. These machines take all the hard work out of log splitting by driving a wedge slowly into the log, which is held in place by a metal frame. The force of these machines is so great that even the most difficult log splits under this treatment.

Shapes and sizes

Woodsmen tend to split logs to patterns that give a good variety of shapes and sizes to burn, which also helps stacking in the woodshed. Small logs are usually left whole or split in half; larger logs are split into four or six segments.

As an interesting aside, you might notice recently chopped logs glowing in the dark; look out for a bluish-green glow that is created by some fungi in decaying wood. Known as 'foxfire', it is believed that the light attracts insects to spread spores or acts as a warning to hungry animals.

Making kindling

Choose a wood that is easy to ignite – softwoods such as pine or perhaps ash are good – and select a log with few knots in it. Use a hatchet to

The use of wedges and a sledgehammer to split logs.

A hydraulic ram log splitter.

chop the log into small pieces, perhaps 10–20mm in diameter. You can chop a year's supply of kindling, which will season much faster than a larger log. Or you might opt to have a chopping log and hatchet near your stove and chop kindling as needed. Regardless of when and how you make your kindling, above all it needs to be dry. Bits of bark also work well, as do twigs collected in winter and dried over the summer. Dried pine cones make excellent kindling, smell nice when burning, and a basket full by the stove looks great too!

Storing firewood

Two essential rules when seasoning your firewood are to keep rain off the logs and allow a good airflow through them. By far the best way of achieving this is to erect a purpose-made woodshed. Some people are tempted to store freshly delivered logs into the corner of an almost airtight garden shed or a damp outbuilding and close the door. At best these logs will dry very slowly and at worst they will rot.

In the overall planning to fit a wood-burning stove, you should carefully consider where you intend to store your wood and the space it requires – two years' worth of firewood can take up a fair amount of space.

Woodsheds

Your woodshed should be user-friendly and conveniently close to your house, as eventually you need to carry every piece of firewood from the woodshed to your stove. Site the shed where it gets a good flow of air – ideally somewhere south-facing so that the sun can get to the wood – and make sure the base is either raised off the ground or dry and well drained, as the wood shouldn't be sitting in water.

The size of woodshed you need depends on how often you use your stove, for how long, how many rooms you are heating and how you source your wood. If you run a 5kW stove for 2–4 hours, seven days a week, then (assuming that the wood is at 25 per cent moisture) you would use about 1–1.5 tonnes of wood per year, depending on the type of wood. For example, one tonne of dense hardwood logs, like oak, stored in a random, thrown-type of woodshed, would take up around 4m^3; softwood logs, like larch, stored in the same way would take up

An example of a woodshed showing two bays, one for seasoning and one for using now.

around 5.5m³.

It is always better to build a woodshed that is slightly bigger than you think you need. What makes most sense is a woodshed with two generous bays, one for the wood that you are currently using and the other for the wood that you are seasoning ready for use next winter. Trying to manage the seasoning and storing of your firewood in a small woodshed is very difficult, as it is hard to segregate the fresh logs from those that have been in the woodshed for some time. So for two years' worth of firewood, you should aim for two bays, each allowing for at least 4m³ for dense hardwood, 5.5m³ for softwood.

If you don't season your own firewood but get regular deliveries, you need less space – around 2m³ is probably plenty. Some suppliers may provide a woodshed stacking or filling service at a charge, or you may be willing to do this yourself; siting your woodshed close to where your supplier delivers can save time and effort. Does your supplier have a tipping flatbed truck? If so, can you design your woodshed so that they can simply tip a load into it?

A woodshed needs to be little more than a roof with three slatted sides. The front should be open for easy working both within the shed and for unloading and stacking the logs. Stacked firewood takes up significantly less room than firewood just thrown in a heap, but if you have the space to simply store them in a heap it saves a lot of time. If this is the case, design front boards to hold back the wood. A simple way to do this is to use two vertical boards with a spacer either side to form a groove, then slot each end of your front boards into this groove as needed. As you pile on more wood you simply add more boards. The addition of a small extra piece of wood on the lower side of each end of the board creates an air gap between them.

Your woodshed should have a base to prevent the firewood from lying in contact with bare earth, as any logs touching the ground absorb moisture, which could promote rotting. A firm, dry base of concrete is fine but make sure there is some slope so that puddles don't form beneath the logs. A free-draining base may be best and this could be either stout paving slabs on sand or coarse gravel (say, 25–50mm). In both cases make sure that they are resting on a tough permeable membrane. This prevents soil from migrating into the sand or gravel and reducing its drying effectiveness; it also helps to prevent weed growth. Any weeds in or around your woodshed slow airflow and reduce the shed's effectiveness at drying logs.

Other storage options

Tarpaulins

A tarpaulin can be used to store and protect firewood or if space is really limited. However, a great deal of wood is ruined by poor use of a tarpaulin so only use one as a temporary measure and, again, ensure the logs are not in direct contact with the ground by providing a suitable base – for example, one made of pallets. The tarpaulin you buy should be of good quality. Once the wood is stacked on its base, pull the tarpaulin tightly over the logs and secure it against the wind. Placing bricks on the top and against the sides often creates puddles, so tie the tarpaulin down using the eyelets around the edges. Avoid bringing the sides right down to the ground so that air can flow freely through your woodpile.

Mesh-sided dumpy bags

If you have enough space, another effective way to season and store wood is to use mesh-sided dumpy bags. Lay a pallet on the ground, put the dumpy bag on it and fill it with chopped logs. Other dumpy bags can be placed beside the first, leaving a gap for good airflow. Once complete, cover with a roof of corrugated iron or similar, making sure you have a good roof overhang so the sides of the bags don't get wet, then leave to dry. An advantage of dumpy bags is that a whole bag can be moved at a time with a pallet truck (or front-end loader if you have the luxury). Stillages, such as wooden potato crates or roof slate crates, make a good alternative to mesh-sided dumpy bags. They are slotted, so they let air through, and are easy to stack.

Lean-to woodsheds

A lean-to woodshed against the south- or, failing that, west-facing elevation of a house or an outbuilding can also be a suitable way of storing wood. The back wall is already built, which may save space while also allowing you to site the shed closer to the door you have to carry the wood through.

Pallets

If you are counting the pounds, or simply object to unnecessary expense, pallets are a quick and easy way to make a woodshed. Use one on the ground and then three more for the sides and back. Break a few pallets apart and used these extra pieces of wood to form a raised, pitched roof.

Wood stacks

It is possible to season wood by simply stacking it outside with a light covering on top, or at least to start the process this way. In Scandinavia you may see large round stacks of self-supporting firewood; in forests in the UK, you may see stacks of long logs undergoing initial seasoning before they are split. These straight stacks are typically raised off the ground on a couple of branches used as bearers, with either a stake or a tree at each end as a support.

Stacking your firewood can help maximise the amount you can fit in, but remember to make it safe: you don't want an avalanche of logs as you collect fresh supplies! Stacking firewood logs is a little like building a drystone wall; every log is a different size or shape and you must think how it best fits into the stack. Use the big, heavy, split logs to make the corners, interlocking them and using their weight to make the corner stable. Laying the logs on the edges of the wood stack (the outside wall) so that they are slightly sloping downwards and outwards allows them to drain off any rain and prevents rain from entering the stack. Ancient drystone buildings were made in this way; stones were laid sloping slightly outwards to prevent rain from entering the building.

A halfway house is to build a wall of stacked logs at the front of your woodshed one or two logs thick, which holds back the logs further, then simply throw other logs in at random.

Aim to store at least a day's worth of wood right by your stove – ideally more so the stack only needs replenishing weekly. A day's worth is likely to be around half to one wheelbarrow of wood, but that depends on the size of your stove and how you use it. The wood will also dry a little further while stored inside. Many people use a log basket but you might consider building an alcove into a wall. Finally, it's worth thinking about the route you'll use to bring the wood inside – make it as short as possible to save you time in the long run.

The smallest multi-fuel stove in the Newbourne Range 35FS 4kW, making it ideal for installation into small fireplaces and today's smaller homes.

Although small in size, it is big in features with 80% efficiency, stylish good looks and excellent heat output. A full size curved door and large viewing window gives an impressive view of the fire burning beautifully yet efficiently in the fire chamber. With a portrait design, the stove is ideal for installation in canal boats, townhouses or country cottages, and fits a minimum fireplace opening of 18" x 26" height, whether installed into a fireplace or a free-standing situation, to warm your home and heart.

  A World of Stoves, A World of Choice

Tel: +44 (0) 1473 736399 • Fax: +44 (0) 1473 736406
email: sales@woodstoves.co.uk • www.woodstoves.co.uk

Don't forget to get it swept!

Choosing a Guild sweep means they:

- ▶ Meet the Industry Standard
- ▶ Are fully trained, certified & registered
- ▶ Have correct insurance cover
- ▶ Provide nationally recognised sweeping certificates
- ▶ Offer expert help and advice
- ▶ Quality service from quality professionals.

www.guildofmasterchimneysweeps.co.uk

Appendices...................................... 141

APPENDICES

" " *Stoves are now being made which can be connected to an external air supply, which is essential as our houses become more and more airtight.* " "

LEFT: *Morsø 6140 wood-burning stove.*

STOVES ONLINE

Get *The Stove Book* for FREE!

With so many different types of stoves and chimneys to choose from, it can be difficult knowing exactly which one will best suit your situation.

Anyone who has visited the Stovesonline website will know that we are all about giving people the necessary information so that they can make the right choice for themselves.

So we are really pleased to see the publication of a clear and informative book that cuts through all the hype and technical jargon and tells you, in plain English, exactly what you need to know.

The Stove Book helps you find the wood-burning stove that you really wanted, and tells you exactly what is going to be needed to get it installed, and so makes our lives easier in helping you to do that.

So if you have bought this book then we will give you back the purchase price when you come to us to buy your stove. Simply quote the number on the reverse of this card. This will be in addition to all the normal Stovesonline discounts.

Morsø 7940

We have the widest selection of wood and multi-fuel stoves available in the country and can supply everything you'll need to get your stove fitted and burning well. Most models are in stock and can be delivered to you within 24 hours.

Our experienced technical team can advise you on every aspect of choosing your stove and designing the chimney. Once the stove has arrived, our team will gladly help with how it should be installed and advise on its day-to-day running.

If you need to find a properly qualified and experienced fitter then our national installer database is available to all our customers, enabling us to put you in touch with the right local installer.

To get the purchase price of this book taken off the cost of your stove purchase, simply quote this number: 10772

Esse 200 XK

Stove manufacturers and distributors

AAROW
Arada
The Fireworks, Weycroft Avenue, Axminster, Devon, EX13 5HU
Tel: 01297 35700
www.aradastoves.com

ACR
UK distributor:
ACR Heat Products
Unit 1, Weston Works, Weston Lane, Birmingham, B11 3RP
Tel: 0121 706 8266
www.acrheatproducts.com

ADURO
UK distributor: Fire Product Distribution
Taymin Business Park, Mitcham Road, Blackpool, FY4 4QN
Tel: 0845 226 0576
www.fireproduct distribution.com

AGA RANGEMASTER
Station Road, Ketley, Telford, Shropshire,
TF1 5AQ
Tel: 0845 381365
www.agaliving.com

AGA RAYBURN
Station Road, Ketley, Telford, Shropshire,
TF1 5AQ
Tel: 0845 7626147
www.rayburn-web.co.uk

AMESTI
UK distributor:
Gardeco
PO Box 5500, Kidderminster, DY11 9BB
Tel: 0870 2340003
www.gardeco.co.uk

ARADA
The Fireworks, Weycroft Avenue, Axminster, Devon, EX13 5HU.
Tel: 01297 35700
www.aradastoves.com

AUSTROFLAMM
UK distributor:
Fireplace Products
Eva (UK) Ltd, Lower Barn Farm, Rayleigh, Essex, SS6 9ET
Tel: 0845 3455 496
www.fireplaceproducts. co.uk

BARBAS
PO BOX 6940, Kidderminster, DY11 9EW
Tel: 01562 515715
www.interfocos.com

BODART and GONAY
UK Distributor: Lloyds Heat Design
32-36 Intake Road, Bolsover Business Park, Bolsover, S44 6BB
Tel: 01246 828 942
www.lloyds.uk.com

BOHEMIA
UK distributor: Pevex
Unit 12F Seven Acres, Business Park, Newbourne Road, Waldringfield, Nr Woodbridge, Suffolk, IP12 4PS
Tel: 01473 736399
www.woodstoves.co.uk

BROSELEY
Broseley Fires Ltd
Knights Way, Battlefield Enterprise Park, Shrewsbury, Shropshire, SY1 3AB
Tel: 01743 461444
www.broseleyfires.com

BRUNO
UK Distributor:
Stovesonline Ltd
Capton, Dartmouth, Devon, TQ6 OJE
Tel: 01845 2265754
www.stovesonline.co.uk

BURLEY
Lands' End Way, Oakham, Rutland, LE15 6RB
Tel: 01572 756956
www.burley.co.uk

CARRON
Hurlingham Business Park, Fulbeck Heath, Grantham, Lincolnshire, NG32 3HL
Tel: 0808 129 2224
www.carron.uk.net

CAPITAL FIREPLACES
Units 12-17
Henlow Trading Estate,
Henlow SG16 6DS
Tel: 01462 813138
www.capitalfireplaces.
co.uk

CAST TECH
East Side, Tyne Dock, South
Shields, NE33 5SP
Tel: 0191 497 4280
www.casttec.co.uk

CHARNWOOD
UK distributor:
AJ Wells & Sons
Bishops Way, Newport, Isle
of Wight, TF1 5AQ
Tel: 01983 537777
www.charnwood.com

CHESNEY
194 - 200 Battersea Park
Road, London, SW11 4ND
Tel: 020 7627 1410
www.chesneys.co.uk

CLEARVIEW
More Works, Bishops Castle,
Shropshire, SY9 5HH
Tel: 01588 650401
www.clearviewstoves.com

CONTURA
Box 134 , Skulptörvägen 10
285 23 Markaryd, Sweden
Tel: +00 46(0) 433 75100
brasvarme@contura.se

COUNTRY KILN
Waterlands, Fenwick Road,
Stewarton, Ayrshire,
KA3 5JE
Tel: 01560 483966
www.woodburningstoves
limited.com

DE MANINCOR
UK distributor:
Firepower Heating
Units 11 & 12, Quadrant
Distribution Centre,
Quedgeley, Gloucester,
GL2 2RN
Tel: 01803 712735
www.aquathermstoves.
co.uk

DIK GEURTS
UK Distributor:
Drugasar Ltd
Deans Road, Swinton,
Manchester M27 0JH, UK
Tel: 0161 793 8700
www.drugasar.co.uk

DIMPLEX
Millbrook House, Grange
Drive, Hedge End,
Southampton, Hants,
SO30 2DF
Tel: 0844 879 3589
www.dimplex.co.uk

DOVRE
UK distributor:
Stovax Ltd
Falcon Road, Sowton
Industrial Estate, Exeter,
Devon, EX2 7LF
Tel: 01392 474000
www.dovre.co.uk

DOWLING
Unit 3, Bladnoch Bridge
Estate, Newton Stewart,
Scotland DG8 9AB
Tel: 01988 402666
www.dowlingstoves.com

DROOF KAMINOFEN
UK distributor:
MMF Ltd
Flue House, 55 Woodburn

Road, Smethwick,
West Midlands, B66 2PU
Tel: 0121 5556555
www.drooffstoves.com

DRU FIRES
UK Distributor: Drugasar
Deans Road, Swinton,
Manchester, M27 0JH
Tel: 0161 793 8700
www.drugasar.co.uk

DUNSLEY HEAT
Bridge Mills, Huddersfield
Road, Holmfirth,
Nr Huddersfield, West
Yorkshire, HD9 3TW
Tel: 01484 682635
www.dunsleyheat.co.uk

ECCO
Landy Vent (UK) Ltd
Foster House, 2 Redditch Road,
Studley, Warwickshire, B80 7AX
Tel: 01527 857814
www.landyvent.co.uk

EKOL
Station Works, Johns Road,
Wareham, Dorset, BH20 4BG
Tel: 01929 555 211
www.defrastoves.com

ESSE ENGINEERING
Long Ing, Barnoldswick,
Colne, Lancashire,
B18 6BN
Tel: 01282 813235
www.esse.com

EVERGREEN
UK distributor: Stoves
Are Us
Pennine House, Longbow
Close, Huddersfield, West
Yorkshire, HD2 1GQ
Tel: 01484 434321
www.evergreenstoves.co.uk

FIREBELLY
Unit C Ainleys Industrial
Estate, Elland, HX5 9JP
Tel: 01422 375582
www.firebellystoves.com

FIREFOX
UK distributor:
Capital Fireplaces
Units 12-17/Henlow Trading
Estate, Henlow SG16 6DS
Tel: 01462 813138
**www.capitalfireplaces.
co.uk**

FIREPOWER HEATING
Units 11 & 12, Quadrant,
Distribution Centre,
Quedgeley, Gloucester,
GL2 2RN
Tel: 0844 332 0155
**www.firepowerheating.
co.uk**

FONDIS
UK distributor:
Firepower
Units 11 & 12, Quadrant
Distribution Centre,
Quedgeley, Gloucester,
GL2 2RN
Tel: 01803 712735
**www.firepowerheating.
co.uk**

FRANCO BELGE
UK distributor: ACR
Heat Products
Unit 1, Weston Works,
Weston Lane, Tyseley,
Birmingham, B11 3RP
Tel: 0121 7068266
**www.acrheatproducts.
co.uk**

GREENHEART
UK Distributor:
Stovesonline Ltd
Capton, Dartmouth, Devon,
TQ6 OJE
Tel: 01845 2265754
www.stovesonline.co.uk

HAAS and SOHN
UK distributor:
Fire Product
Distribution
Taymin Business Park,
Mitcham Road, Blackpool,
FY4 4QN
Tel: 0845 226 0576
**www.fireproduct
distribution.com**

HARRIE LEENDERS
UK distributor:
Robeys Ltd
Goods Road, Belper,
Derbyshire, DE56 1UU
Tel: 01773 820940
www.robeys.co.uk

HASE-KAMINOFENBAU
UK distributor: Anglia
Fireplaces
Anglia House, Kendal Court,
Cambridge Road,
Trumpington,
Cambridge, CB24 9YS
Tel: 01223 234713
www.fireplaces.co.uk

HEAT DESIGN
60 Hawthorn Road, Western
Industrial Estate, Naas
Road, Dublin 12, Republic
of Ireland
Tel: +(00) 353 14089192
www.tripp.ie

HETA
UK distributor:
Pevex Enterprises Ltd
Business Park, Newbourne
Road, Waldringfield,
Suffolk IP12 4PS
Tel: 01473 736399
www.woodstoves.co.uk

HOTPOD
Tel: 01736 797285
www.hotpod.co.uk

HUNTER
Aspen House, Pynes Hill,
Exeter, Devon, EX2 5AZ
Tel: 01392 422760
www.hunterstoves.co.uk

HWAM
UK distributor
Euroheat
Bishops Frome ,
Worcestershire, WR6 5AY
Tel: 01885 491112
www.euroheat.co.uk

INVICTA
UK distributor: Pevex
Enterprises
Unit 12F, Seven Acres
Business Park, Newbourne
Road, Waldringfield, Nr
Woodbridge, Suffolk,
IP12 4PS
Tel: 01473 736399
www.woodstoves.co.uk

JACOBUS
UK distributor: Landy
Vent (UK)
Foster House, 2 Redditch
Road, Studley,
Warwickshire, B80 7AX
Tel: 01527 857814
www.landyvent.co.uk

JAMES SMELLIE

Unit H, Leona Industrial Estate, Nimmings Road, Halesowen, West Midlands. B62 9JQ
Tel: 0121 5611167
www.jamessmellie.co.uk

JETMASTER

Unit 2, Peacock Trading Centre, Goodwood Road, Eastleigh, Hampshire, SO50 4NT
Tel: 012380 629513
www.jetmaster.co.uk

JØTUL UK

1 The IO Centre, Nash Road, Redditch, Worcestershire, B98 7AS
http://jotul.com/uk/home

KLOVER

UK distributor:
Firepower Heating
Units 11 & 12, Quadrant, Distribution Centre, Quedgeley, Gloucester, GL2 2RN
Tel: 0844 332 0155
www.firepowerheating.co.uk

LANDYVENT

Foster House,
2 Redditch Road, Studley, B80 7AX
Tel: 01527 857 814
www.landyvent.co.uk

LA NORDICA-EXTRAFLAME

Available from retailers: Stovesonline
Capton, Dartmouth, Devon, TQ6 0JE
Tel: 0845 2265754
www.stovesonline.co.uk

LOGFIRE

Britannia House, Junction Street, Darwen, Lancashire, BB3 2RB
Tel: 01254 700204
www.logfirestoves.com

MENDIP

Eurostove, Unit S5, Mendip Industrial Estate, Mendip Road, Somerset, BS26 2UG
Tel: 01934 750500
www.mendipstoves.co.uk

MORSØ UK

Unit 7, The io Centre, Valley Drive, Swift Valley, Rugby, Warwickshire, CV21 1TW
Tel: 01788 554410
www.morsoe.com

NORDPEIS

UK Distributor:
Stovax
Falcon Road, Sowton, Industrial Estate, Exeter, Devon, EX2 7LF
Tel: 01392 474000
www.stovax.com

OAKFIRE

UK distributor:
Stovesonline
Capton, Dartmouth, Devon, TQ6 0JE
Tel: 01845 2265754
www.stovesonline.co.uk

PANADERO

UK distributor: The Marble Warehouse
Maritime Industrial Estate, Maesycoed, Pontypridd, CF37 1NY
Tel: 01443 408548
www.panaderostoves.com

PARKRAY

Aspen House, Pynes Hill, Exeter, Devon, EX2 5AZ
Tel: 01392 422760
www.hunterstoves.co.uk

PEVEX

Unit 12F Seven Acres Business Park, Newbourne Road, Waldringfield, Nr Woodbridge, Suffolk IP12 4PS
Tel: 01473 736399
www.woodstoves.co.uk co.uk

PIAZZETTA

UK distributor: Robeys
Goods Road, Belper, Derbyshire, DE56 1UU
Tel: 01773 820940
www.robeys.co.uk

PORTWAY

UK distributor: BFM Europe
Gordon Banks Drive, Trentham Lakes, Stoke-on-Trent, Staffordshire ST4 4TJ
Tel: 01782 339000
www.bfm-europe.com

PYROCLASSIC FIRES

UK distributor:
Pyroclassic Fires
72 Hill Top Avenue, Cheadle Hulme, Cheshire, SK8 7JA
Tel: 07712 400252
www.pyroclassic.co.uk

RIKA

UK distributor:
Euroheat
Court Farm Business Park, Bishops Frome, Worcestershire, WR6 5AY

Tel: 01885 4951100
www.euroheat.co.uk

RIVA & RIVA VISION

UK distributor: Stovax
Falcon Road, Sowton
Industrial Estate, Exeter,
Devon, EX2 7LF
Tel: 01392 474000
www.stovax.com

ROBEYS

Goods Road, Belper,
Derbyshire, DE56 1UU
Tel: 01773 820940
www.robeys.co.uk

ROFER AND RODI

UK distributor:
Rofer and Rodi
Unit 10, Airedale
Business Centre, Millenium
Road, Skipton, North
Yorkshire, BD32 2TZ
Tel: 01756 700004
www.rofer.co.uk

SAEY

UK Distributor:
Eurostove
Unit H1, Mendip
Industrial, Estate, Mendip
Road, Rooksbridge,
Somerset, BS26 2UG
Tel: 01934 750500
www.eurostove.co.uk

SALAMANDER

Rosemount, Canada Hill,
Ogwell, Devon
TQ12 6AF
Tel: 01626 363507
www.salamanderstoves.com

SCAN

UK Distributor:

Jøtul UK Ltd
1 The io Centre, Nash Road,
Park Farm North, Redditch
Worcestershire B98 7AS
http://scan.dk/uk

SCANTHERM

UK Distributor:
Encompass
The Pool Room, Standsted
House, Rowlands Castle
Hants, PO9 6DX
Tel: 02392 410045
www.encompassco.com

SIRIUS

UK distributor:
Capital Fireplaces
Units 12-17/Henlow Trading
Estate, Henlow SG16 6DS
Tel: 01462 813138
www.capitalfireplaces.co.uk

SNUG

Stovesonline Ltd
Capton, Dartmouth,
Devon, TQ6 OJE
Tel: 01845 2265754
www.stovesonline.co.uk

STOVAX

Falcon Road, Sowton
Industrial Estate, Exeter,
Devon, EX2 7LF
Tel: 01392 474000
www.stovax.com

Stovesonline

Capton, Dartmouth,
Devon, TQ6 OJE
Tel: 01845 2265754
www.stovesonline.co.uk

STRATFORD

UK distributor:
Arada
The Fireworks, Weycroft

Avenue, Axminster, Devon,
EX13 5HU.
Tel: 01297 35700
www.aradastoves.com

SUPRA

UK distributor: Fire
Product Distribution
Taymin Business Park,
Mitcham Road, Blackpool,
FY4 4QN
Tel: 0845 226 0576
www.fireproduct
distribution.com

TERMATECH

UK distributor:
Specflue
8 Curzon Road, Chilton
Industrial Estate, Sudbury,
Suffolk, CO10 2XW
Tel: 0800 9020220 W
www.termatech.co.uk

TIGER

UK distributor:
Capital Fireplaces
Units 12-17/Henlow Trading
Estate, Henlow SG16 6DS
Tel: 01462 813138
www.capitalfireplaces.co.uk

TOWN AND COUNTRY

Town & Country Fires

1 Enterprise Way, Thornton
Road Industrial Estate,
Pickering, North Yorkshire
YO18 7NA
Tel: 01751 474 803
www.townandcountry
fires.co.uk

VARDE

UK distributor: Stovax
Falcon Road, Sowton

Industrial Estate, Exeter,
Devon, EX2 7LF
Tel: 01392 474000
www.stovax.com

VERMONT CASTINGS
UK distributor: ACR
Heat Products
Unit 1 Weston Works,
Weston Lane, Birmingham,
B11 3RP
Tel: 0121 706 8266
www.acrheatproducts.com

VILLAGER
UK distributor: Arada
The Fireworks, Weycroft
Avenue, Axminster, Devon,
EX13 5HU.
Tel: 01297 35700
www.aradastoves.com

WALLNOEFER
UK distributor:
Firepower Heating
Units 11 & 12, Quadrant,
Distribution Centre,
Quedgeley, Gloucester,
GL2 2RN
Tel: 0844 332 0155
www.firepowerheating.
co.uk

WANDERS
UK distributor:
Firepower Heating
Units 11 & 12, Quadrant,
Distribution Centre,
Quedgeley, Gloucester,
GL2 2RN
Tel: 0844 332 0155
www.firepowerheating.
co.uk

WATERFORD STANLEY
Unit 401- 403,
Waterford Industrial Estate,
Cork Road, Waterford,
Republic of Ireland
www.waterfordstanley.
com

WESTFIRE
Eurostove
Unit H1, Mendip Industrial
Estate, Mendip Road,
Rooksbridge, Somerset,
BS26 2UG
Tel: 01934 750500
www.eurostove.co.uk

WOODFIRE
Firepower Heating
Units 11 & 12, Quadrant,
Distribution Centre,
Quedgeley, Gloucester,
GL2 2RN
Tel: 0844 332 0155
www.firepowerheating.
co.uk

WOODWARM
Metal Developments
The Workshop, Wheatcroft
Farm, Cullompton, Devon
EX151RA
Tel: 01884 35806
www.woodwarmstoves.
co.uk

YEOMAN
Yeoman Stoves,
Falcon Road, Sowton
Industrial Estate
Exeter, Devon, EX2 7LF
www.yeomanstoves.co.uk

Resources

Organisations

Association of Plumbing and Heating Contractors (APHC)
www.aphc.co.uk

British Flue and Chimney Manufacturers' Association
www.bfcma.co.uk

Building Engineering Services Competence Assessment (BESCA)
www.besca.org.uk

Defra (The Department for Environment and Rural Affairs)
http://smokecontrol.defra.gov.uk

Energy Saving Trust
www.energysavingtrust.co.uk

Forestry Commission
www.forestresearch.gov.uk/fr/woodfuel

Guild of Master Chimney Sweeps
www.guildofmasterchimneysweeps.co.uk

National Association for Professional Inspectors and Testers
(NAPIT) **www.napit.org.uk**

National Inspection Council for Electrical Installation Contracting
(NICEIC)
www.niceic.com

Ofgem
https://www.ofgem.gov.uk/

Small Woods Association
www.smallwoods.org.uk

Stove Industry Alliance
www.stoveindustryalliance.com

Stove reviews
www.whatstove.co.uk

The Forest Stewardship Council
www.fsc-uk.org

The Royal Forestry Society (RFS)
www.rfs.org.uk

WoodSure
www.woodsure.co.uk/suppliers.htm

Woodland Management
www.sylva.org.uk/myforest

Passivhaus UK
www.passivhaus.org.uk

Schemes and regulations

Heating Equipment Testing and Approval Scheme (HETAS)
www.hetas.co.uk/find-fuels/
HETAS is the official body recognised by the government to approve biomass and solid fuel domestic heating appliances, fuels and services, including the registration of competent installers and servicing businesses. The website includes a directory of accredited producers and suppliers.

Microgeneration Certificate Scheme (MCS)
www.microgenerationcertification.org/
The Microgeneration Certification Scheme (MCS) is an internationally recognised quality assurance scheme supported by the Department of Energy & Climate Change (DECC). The MCS certifies microgeneration technologies used to produce electricity and heat from renewable sources. The MCS is also an eligibility requirement for the government's financial incentives, which include the Renewable Heat Incentive (RHI). The Installer Search area of the website enables you to search for an MCS-accredited installer in your area.

Renewable Heat Incentive (RHI)
www.gov.uk/government/policies/increasing-the-use-of-low-carbon-technologies/supporting-pages/renewable-heat-incentive-rhi
The Renewable Heat Incentive (RHI) is the government's long-term financial support programme for renewable heat technologies. The Domestic RHI is open to homeowners, private landlords, social landlords and self-builders. The Non-domestic RHI provides payments to industry, businesses and public sector organisations.

UK Smoke Control Areas – Defra UK
http://smokecontrol.defra.gov.uk/Planning Portal

Planning Portal
www.planningportal.gov.uk
The latest version of the Approved Document J can be downloaded from this site.

Resources

Green Building Press
PO Box 32, Llandysul
Carmarthenshire
Wales
SA44 5ZA
www.greenbuildingpress.co.uk/
Publishers of the *Green Building Magazine* and other green publications. Website also contains a forum, where members comment and discuss all aspects of green building.

Forestry Commission
'*A Woodfuel Strategy for England*' – available online as a PDF:
www.forestry.gov.uk/pdf/fce-woodfuel-strategy.pdf/$FILE/fce-wood-fuel-strategy.pdf
Woodland management books…?

Glossary

Airwash – Air that is drawn in over the glass which helps to keep the glass clean as well as providing secondary air to the fire.

Ash pan – The receptacle for catching the ash that comes through the grate.

Auger – The screw conveyor that lifts pellets from the hopper and drops them into the crucible in a wood pellet stove.

Baffle – A plate positioned near the top of the firebox and designed to divert the hot gases to the sides, and so increase the heat taken from them, before they leave the stove.

Biomass – Plant based fuel.

Boiler stove – A stove that is designed to heat water to provided central heating and/or domestic hot water.

Chimney cowl – The terminal put on top of a chimney, usually to keep rain out but some also prevent downdraft, keep birds out etc.

Combustion air – The air required by the stove to burn the fuel.

Conduction – In this context this is the movement of heat through the walls of a stove.

Convection – In this context convection refers to the movement of air as it picks up heat from a stove.

Convecting Stove – A stove designed to give some radiant heat and some convected warmth. A convecting stove normally has double walls which draw up cool air between them and then spread that warm air around the room.

Dew point – The temperature at which solids start to condense out of the smoke, leaving tar and soot in the chimney. Flues should normally be working above this temperature.

Downdraught – Certain conditions around a chimney can cause smoke to momentarily stop being drawn up, or even be pushed back down. The moment that happens smoke is puffed into the room.

Dry stove – non-boiler stove.

External air supply – where some or all of the air needed for the stove's combustion is ducted directly into the stove from the outside.

Fire bricks – the lining inside a stove's firebox that both protects the walls of the stove and raises the firebox temperature to ensure a clean burn.

Firebox – The chamber in the stove where the combustion takes places.

Flaunching – the sloping fillet of cement or mortar embedding the base of a chimney pot.

Grate – The grid or bars in the base of the firebox that allow air up through and ash to drop down. Grates are normally made from cast iron.

Green wood – wood that has yet to be fully seasoned so that the moisture content is still too high (greater than 25%) for burning.

Hardwood – Wood from broadleaved trees.

Heartwood – the dense inner part of the tree.

Heat load calculation – Calculating the amount of heat that is needed to maintain a house at a comfortable living temperature.

Heat pump – A appliance that transfers heat from a colder area to a hotter area. In house heating terms it is basically a fridge working in reverse.

Iinfrared waves – radiation that involves waves rather than particles. It is the warmth you feel on your skin when you are near a stove.

Inset or insert stove – A stove that is built into the wall or a chamber as opposed to a freestanding stove.

Kindling – thin dry pieces of wood that will burn easily and are used to start a fire.

Leca – Lightweight expanded clay granules

that are used to insulate around a liner in a chimney.

Linertherm – A heatproof insulating mat that is wrapped around a flexible liner to maintain the temperature of the flue gases as they go up the chimney.

Masonry stove – A heavy ceramic tiled stove that stores heat in its masonry mass and emits it slowly .

Moisture content – The amount of water still retained by firewood. When using a moisture meter one should be aiming for a moisture content of 25% or less.

Moisture meter – a meter used to measure the water content of firewood

Multifuel stove – A stove that is designed to burn wood and coal.

MVHR – mechanical ventilation with heat recovery.

Nominal heat output – The heat output that a stove has been tested to.

Passivhaus – A building that has been highly insulated and draft proved so that it requires very little energy to heat it.

Pellet stove – An automated stove that burns wood pellets.

Primary air – Air that is brought into the stove below the fire.

Riddling – Agitating the grate to encourage the ash to fall through.

Rock-wool sleeve – A sleeve of rockwool, usually with a foil backing, that is used to maintain the flue gas temperature in a flexible liner.

Sapwood – The less dense outer layer of the wood between the heartwood and the bark.

Seasoned – wood that has been brought down to a moisture content of below 25%.

Secondary air supply – Air that is brought in above the fire.

Secondary combustion – When the gases given off by the fire are burnt further up in the firebox.

Slow or slumber-burning – Where the combustion air going into the stove is restricted and makes the fire burn slowly. Slumber burning is normally inefficient and smoky.

Smoke control areas – Areas in many of our cities where only certain fuels are allowed to be burnt. Stoves can be tested to show that they can burn wood sufficiently cleanly as to be allowed to burn wood in those areas.

Softwood – Wood from conifers.

Tertiary air supply – A third supply of air, usually brought in through a row of holes in the back wall of the firebox. This extra supply of air normally results in an even cleaner and more efficient burn.

Thermal store – A highly insulated tank designed to store heat from a stove or solar panel until it is required.

Thermalux – Highly insulating and fireproof structural boards that are used to construct chambers for insert stoves and chimney breasts.

Thermoelectric effect – direct conversion of temperature differences to electric voltage and vice versa.

Thermo-syphoning – Where the water from a stove can flow around a system without using a pump. It works on the principle that hot water is lighter than cold water.

Vented / unvented heating system – A vented central heating system is an open system that has a small tank that the water expands into as it warms up. An unvented, or pressurised, system is completely sealed and takes care of the expansion using an expansion vessel.

Vermiculite – An insulating material that can be used around stoves and liners.

Wet stove - A stove with a boiler.

Wood gasification stove – A stove that is designed to maximise secondary combustion, ie the burning of any gases given off from the fire.

Index